1st AIR CAVALRY in VIETNAM
The 'First Team'

Simon Dunstan

Ian Allan
PUBLISHING

'The will to win, the will to survive, they endure.
They are more important than the events that occasion them.'
Vince Lombardi – Coach Green Bay Packers

'Nothing is more precious than freedom and independence.'
Ho Chi Minh – President Democratic Republic of Vietnam

First published 2004

ISBN 0 7110 3042 1

© Compendium Publishing Ltd, 2004

Published by Ian Allan Publishing Ltd

an imprint of Ian Allan Publishing Ltd, Hersham, Surrey KT12 4RG
Printed in England by
Ian Allan Printing Ltd, Hersham, Surrey KT12 4RG

Code: 0410/

British Library Cataloguing in Publication Data
A CIP catalogue record for this book is available from the British Library

Note: Website information provided in the Reference section was correct when provided by the author. The publisher can accept no responsibility for this information becoming incorrect.

Acknowledgements
Design: Compendium Design
Maps and artwork: Mark Franklin

1st Cavalry Division Fort Hood TX
William Harry Boudreau
Cavalry Outpost Publications.
Robin Cross
Steven C. Draper – Director/Curator 1st Cavalry Division Fort Hood, TX
First Cavalry Division Association
Kevin Lyles
NARA
Martin Pegler
Ralph Young
Steve Zaloga

the photographs on pages 61 and 63 are reproduced courtesy of Kevin Lyles and Tony Mottram.

Many of the photographs reproduced in this book clearly do not portray the correct colours. Shot 30 years ago on print film, the colours have deteriorated. Nevertheless, we feel that some colour is better than reproducing them in black and white.

◄ S P E A R H E A D ►

1st AIR CAVALRY in VIETNAM
The 'First Team'

An officer and his RTO radioman monitor the arrival
of a flight of UH-1D Hueys as they come in to land to
pick up troops for yet another 'search and destroy'
operation. *National Archives*

CONTENTS

GLOSSARY

1/5th	1st Battalion 5th Cavalry Regiment
AHC	Assault helicopter company
AMTF	Airmobile Task Force
ARA	Aerial rocket artillery
ARVN	Army of the Republic of Vietnam
'Blues'	Rifle platoons
Bn	Battalion
Bty	Battery
Co	Company
C&C	Command and control
CTZ	Corps tactical zones
DEROS	Date Eligible for Return from Overseas
DMZ	Demilitarized zone
FFAR	Free flight aerial rocket
FOO	Forward observation officer
IMR	Improved military rifle
KIA	Killed in action
LAW	Light anti-tank weapon
LZ	Landing zone
LOH	Light observation helicopter
Loach	Hughes OH-6A Cayuse
MACV	Military Assistance Command Vietnam
MLCE	Modernized load-carrying equipment
NVA	North Vietnamese Army
Pink Team	A scout helicopter and a gunship
PZ	Pickup zone
Red Team	Two gunships
Regt	Regiment
RPG	Rocket-propelled grenade
Sqn	Squadron
TAC	Tactical air control
VC	Viet Cong
White Team	Two scout helicopters
WIA	Wounded in action
WP	White Phosphorous

ORIGINS & HISTORY

The enduring image of the US Army cavalryman is ingrained in the public consciousness through a thousand Hollywood movies that have made the horse soldier the stuff of legend in the history of the Wild West. Following their widespread service during the American Civil War under such dynamic leaders as Nathan Bedford Forrest, Phil Sheridan and Jeb Stuart, US cavalry regiments proved indispensable during the expansion of the United States westwards in the late 1860s and 70s. Their primary task was to protect settlers and pioneers as they ventured deep into the hinterland beyond the Mississippi/Missouri River. At the same time, the army was required to safeguard the interests of the native North American Indian nations herded into ever-diminishing reservations as more and more white farmers, trappers and prospectors encroached on their traditional hunting grounds and tribal lands. It was an impossible dichotomy and the army's role essentially became the pacification of the Indian peoples by coercion or force as necessary.

Nevertheless, the first antecedent unit of the 1st Cavalry Division (Airmobile) was formed as early as 1855 when the 2nd Cavalry Regiment was raised as the army was expanded from 10,000 to 15,000 men.[1] In 1861, this unit was redesignated as the 5th Cavalry Regiment. During the Civil War it fought in several famous battles including Bull Run, Antietam, Gettysburg and Appomattox. The 5th together with the 7th, 8th and 9th Cavalry Regiments that remain with the 1st Cavalry Division to this day, fought throughout the Indian Wars against the fearsome fighters of the Sioux, Comanche, Apache, Arapaho, Kiowa and Ute nations culminating in the death of the legendary Chief Sitting Bull and the Battle of Wounded Knee in December 1890.[2] With the crushing of the Oglala Sioux and the Ghost Dance cult, the Indian Wars ended and to the strains of their bugles playing 'Garry Owen', the 7th Cavalry marched ever westwards until their patrols reached the Pacific coast and the frozen tundra of Alaska. The United States of America now stretched from ocean to ocean.

When not acting as policemen during labour disputes, cavalry units fought in the Spanish-American War of 1898 and, in the same year, the 'Buffalo Soldiers' of the 9th Cavalry joined in the famous attack on San Juan Hill with Teddy Roosevelt's 'Rough Riders' in Cuba. Cavalry saw extensive service in the Philippines over the coming years but the majority of horsed units spent most of their time in the sun-scorched deserts of the south-western United States patrolling the border with Mexico. Following an attack by the bandit cum Mexican nationalist Pancho Villa on the town of Columbus, New Mexico, in March 1916, the US Army was directed to mount a punitive expedition into Mexico to capture Villa, dead or alive. Under the command of General 'Black Jack' Pershing, the 5th and 7th Cavalry made up part of the expeditionary force that included two thirds of the entire US air force (eight out of the 13 Curtis JN-2 'Jennies' in service). For the next 11 months and often living off the land, the cavalry units of the Punitive Expedition pursued Pancho Villa and his raiders across northern Mexico in the last great

Notes

1 The 1st Regiment of Dragoons was raised in 1833 and subsequently became the 1st Cavalry Regiment that served in the 1st Cavalry Division between 1921 and 1933.

2 The 7th, 8th and 9th Cavalry Regiments were raised in 1866 with the 12th in 1901.

cavalry campaign conducted by the US Army. On 5 February 1917, Pershing's men returned across the border having surmounted many problems and learnt new lessons in warfare. There were now more pressing commitments. On the next day, the United States joined the war against the Kaiser's Germany and troops were needed on the Western Front.

The Great War was the nemesis of horsed cavalry: the age of the tank had dawned. The great majority of US Army cavalry regiments remained in America patrolling the border with Mexico. Following the war, the cavalry arm was cut from 17 to 14 regiments. With the promulgation of the National Defense Act, the 1st Cavalry Division was formally activated at Fort Bliss, Texas, on 13 September 1921 with Maj Gen Robert Lee Howze as its first division commander. Howze was a seasoned veteran of virtually every cavalry campaign back to the Indian Wars and a recipient of the Medal of Honor. Among the units assigned to the 1st Cavalry Division were the 1st, 7th, 8th and 10th Cavalry Regiments, while the 5th Cavalry joined on 18 December 1922 replacing the 10th. On 3 January 1933, the 12th Cavalry Regiment joined the 1st Cavalry Division and relieved the 1st Cavalry to bring together the principal units within the division of the Vietnam era.[3] Life between the wars was predominantly taken up with border patrols and polo with only two cavalry regiments of the US Army becoming mechanised by 1938. Although experiments were undertaken with armoured scout cars from 1928 onwards, the 1st Cavalry Division remained firmly wedded to the horse.

After the outbreak of war following the Japanese attack on Pearl Harbor, the 1st Cavalry Division was assembled in its entirety at Fort Bliss for extensive field training. Its authorised strength rose from 3,575 to 10,110 troops. In March 1942, the office of Chief of Cavalry was eliminated by the War Department. The 1st Cavalry Division was living on borrowed time as it continued its well-worn path of border surveillance with horses and armoured cars. The horse soldiers were finally dismounted in February 1943. Many cavalrymen resented trading in their saddles to become 'cushion pounders'. However, they were allowed some memories of their glorious past with the retention of of the term 'Troops' where the infantry used 'companies' and soldiers remained 'Troopers' while proudly wearing yellow cavalry insignia and marching beneath the red and white guidons of the former horse regiments. The division was retrained as amphibious assault infantry for service in the Pacific War, departing overseas on 23 May 1943.

After six months training in the jungles of Queensland in Australia, the division was ready for battle. On 29 February 1944, the 1st Cavalry Division set sail for the Admiralty Islands and stormed ashore in an amphibious assault on Los Negros. Harking back to their involvement in the Plains Wars, the division incorporated a unique radio unit known as the 'Code Talkers' with Lakota and Dakota native American Indians who communicated with other units in the ancient tribal Sioux language that defied all enemy radio intercept attempts. After the Admiralty Islands campaign, the division joined the invasion force of the Philippines, landing on Leyte on 20 October 1944. Leyte was followed by Luzon in January 1945 when General Douglas MacArthur ordered the division: 'Go to Manila! Go around the Japs, bounce off the Japs, save your men, but get to Manila! Free the internees at Santo Tomas! Take the Malacanan Palace [the Presidential Palace] and the legislative building!' In a flying column, elements of the division cut a swathe through 100 miles of enemy-held territory to be the first US Army unit to enter the Philippine capital of Manila, releasing many Allied POWs: equally satisfactory was the liberation of the San Miguel brewery. After the 'First Team' was the first into Manila, the 1st Cavalry Division was given the honour to lead the Allied Occupational Army into Tokyo at the conclusion of World War 2. It was another notable first for the 'First Team'.

Following the Army Organization Act of 1950,[4] the 1st Cavalry Division was configured as a standard infantry division. It remained on occupation duties in Japan until

Above: A group photograph of Troop C, 3rd Cavalry taken at Fort Davis, Texas, in 1886 shows these troopers in regulation uniforms but still equipped with US Model 1860 light cavalry sabres which were rare at this late date. They are wearing 1883 campaign hats, 1884 fatigue blouses and are armed with US Model 1873 Springfield carbines and Schofield Smith & Wesson revolvers.
(*Fort Davis National Historical Site*)

Notes

3 The 1st Cavalry Division (Airmobile) assigned cavalry units in Vietnam were drawn from the 5th, 7th, 8th, 9th and 12th Cavalry Regiments.

4 On 25 March 1949, the 1st Cavalry Division was reorganised as a Triangular Division. The 5th, 7th and 8th Cavalry Regiments were retained while the 12th Cavalry Regiment was deactivated.

Above: The classic image of US cavalrymen during the Indian Wars with Sergeant J. Bouck and Corporal Sampson of Troop K, 1st Cavalry, at the Crow Agency Montana in late 1887. They feature an interesting combination of official issue and private purchase items such as the gunbelt with hunting knife and civilian slouch hat worn by Bouck (right) while Sampson wears the superannuated Civil War holster. Soon after this photograph was taken, Sampson was killed by Crow renegades. *National Archives*

Right: On the left, the standard divisional shoulder patch; on the right, the subdued patch used during the Vietnam era.

the communist invasion of South Korea by its northern neighbour on 25 June 1950. Although severely understrength as many specialist personnel and NCOs were immediately despatched to the fighting, the division was deployed piecemeal to South Korea from 18 July to bolster the hard-pressed perimeter of the 'Pusan Pocket' around the last major seaport in the south. After the front was stabilised, the United Nations counterattacked with MacArthur's brilliant amphibious landings at Inchon near the South Korean capital of Seoul. Pounded unmercifully by airpower, the North Korean army crumbled and the United Nations force forged across the 38th Parallel into North Korea on 9 October 1950. The 1st Cavalry Division gained another first by being the first unit into the North Korean capital of Pyongyang, which was captured on 19 October. The advance continued northwards to the Yalu River and the border with communist China. Then the full weight of the Chinese People's Liberation Army fell upon the overextended United Nations forces. A headlong retreat southwards ensued with heavy losses. On 1 November 1950, the 8th Cavalry Regiment was surrounded and cut off at Unsan by Chinese forces. Hand to hand fighting raged for several days: the 8th lost over half its personnel, either dead or POWs, as well as hundreds of vehicles and weapons.

Ironically, the 1st Cavalry Division was fighting in terrain more suited to horses than vehicles that were restricted to the crumbling tracks and roads in the valley floors. Time and again, the Chinese used sturdy ponies to negotiate the overlooking precipitous hills and outflank UN units. Fierce fighting continued through the bitter winter of 1950/51 until the front lines stabilised along the Han River below Seoul with over 1½ million communist soldiers facing just 250,000 UN troops. During February and March, the 1st Cavalry Division participated in the UN counterattack that recaptured Seoul. After a period in reserve, it returned to the line during the Chinese spring offensive that was thwarted by overwhelming firepower and a dogged UN defence along the Imjin River. The war then became predominantly static along the high ground astride the 38th Parallel as the two sides entered prolonged armistice negotiations at Panmunjon that finally came to fruition on 27 July 1953. Meanwhile, after 18 months of almost continuous fighting,

THE HISTORY OF THE PATCH

The shoulder patch and insignia of the 1st Cavalry Division is one of the most distinctive in the US Army, reflecting the division's proud history and cavalry heritage. Following a War Department directive on the division's formation in 1921, an insignia was designed by Mrs Ben Dorcy, the wife of the colonel then commanding the 7th Cavalry Regiment at Fort Bliss in Texas. As with so many aspects of military history, there are different interpretations as to the original inspiration for the insignia. The background yellow was the traditional colour of the cavalry and a reminder of the golden sunsets at Fort Bliss. The shape was reminiscent of the shield carried by knights in battle. Mrs Dorcy used the yellow cloth of one of her husband's old dress capes as the background for the design. The diagonal bar was originally blue to reflect the other traditional colour of the cavalry from their uniforms. The bar represented a scaling ladder to breach castle walls. In January 1969, Mrs Dorcy wrote to the division to suggest that it could also represent the Jacob's ladder suspended from Chinook helicopters during the Vietnam War. The horse's head was an obvious reference to the cavalry's mounts and was based on the observation of a trooper leading a beautiful black thoroughbred past the Dorsey household. The original specification allowed for only two colours for the divisional insignia due to economic constraints. Subsequently, the blue bar and horse's head were changed to black to represent the colour of iron and armour following mechanisation. With rounded corners and a height of 5¼ inches, the patch is the largest in the US Army and was oversized because, according to Mrs Dorcy, 'the patch had to be large enough to be seen through the dust and sand at Fort Bliss'. During the Vietnam War, the yellow background of the shoulder sleeve insignia was changed to a subdued olive drab for the battle dress uniform in order to minimise the wearer as a potential target to the enemy.

Notes

5 On 1 November 1957, the 1st Cavalry Division was converted to the Pentomic structure with five battle groups. This change brought back the 12th Cavalry Regiment and added the 4th Cavalry Regiment.

6 On 15 July 1963, the new Army Division called Reorganization Objective Army Division or ROAD brought back the triangular divisional structure. For the 1st Cavalry Division this resulted in the loss of the 12th Cavalry Regiment once again as well as the 4th Cavalry Regiment.

Below: Troopers of the 1st Cavalry Division cross the Imjin River on 6 June 1951 aboard M-24 Chaffee light tanks of the divisional reconnaissance company. One of the first US Army formations to see service in the Korean War, the 1st Cavalry Division suffered over 16,000 casualties in 18 months of heavy combat before being withdrawn in to Japan in January 1952.

the 1st Cavalry Division returned to Japan in January 1952 after being relieved by the 45th Infantry Division.

The 1st Cavalry Division remained in Japan until September 1957 when all US forces were redeployed from the main Japanese islands. It then moved to Korea to defend the Demilitarized Zone or DMZ dividing North and South Korea. By now, the 'First Team' was configured as a Pentomic Division[5] of 13,500 men divided into five integrated battle groups that were deemed more suited to the needs of a dispersed nuclear battlefield. With the division's headquarters based at Camp Howze, the 'First Team' spent the next few years patrolling 'Freedom's Frontier' on a 24-hour, seven days a week basis, suffering several fatalities and casualties in clashes with the North Korean border guards. As the only US Army formation in direct contact with the communists (there being no formal end to the Korean War), the 1st Cavalry Division was equipped in 1962 with the full panoply of the new infantry weapons then entering service including M-14 rifles, M-60 general purpose machine guns, M-79 40mm grenade launchers and Claymore anti-personnel mines as well as UH-1A Huey helicopters for front-line medical evacuation. In spring 1963, the division began extensive training with H-19, H-21 and H-37 helicopters in air assault tactics – a role pioneered ten years before during the Korean War.[6] It was a portent of things to come when the 1st Cavalry Division was redeployed to the United States in July 1965; the first time it had returned to America in 22 years. But not for long as another war in Asia was looming large.

READY FOR WAR

THE HOWZE BOARD

Following its successful use during the Korean War for troop lift and resupply on the front lines, the role of the helicopter within the US Army fell by the wayside in the postwar years. The military now concentrated its resources on nuclear weapons and their delivery systems at the expense of conventional forces within the army. However, there remained some firm advocates of the helicopter in war including General Hamilton H. Howze, the Director of Army Aviation. In June 1956, he authorised Colonel Jay D. Vanderpool to form an experimental 'Sky Cavalry' platoon with armed and troop lift helicopters. With like-minded enthusiasts, 'Vanderpool's Fools' conducted several dramatic field exercises to demonstrate the concept of 'vertical envelopment' that was subsequently termed 'airmobility'. Gradually, official approval was gained and the unit was expanded to become the 7292nd Aerial Combat Reconnaissance Company (Provisional) in March 1958.

Two years later, the Rogers Board, chaired by Lt Gen Gordon B. Rogers, was convened to study US Army requirements for all types of aircraft for observation, surveillance and transport. This led to a new generation of helicopters with greatly enhanced performance over existing types thanks largely to the introduction of the compact gas-turbine engine. Rogers also recommended that another board be set up – 'to determine whether the concept of air fighting units was practical and if an experimental unit should be activated to test feasibility and develop material requirements'. This led to the appointment of Lt Gen Hamilton Howze, then the commander of the XVIII Airborne Corps, to head a task force entitled the US Army Tactical Mobility Requirements Board or 'Howze Board' for short.

The revival of interest in the role of the helicopter was now endorsed in high places with the appointment of Secretary of Defense Robert S. McNamara in President John F. Kennedy's administration. A firm believer in a technological solution to military problems, he demanded 'a bold new look at land warfare mobility'. Within a remarkably short time, the Howze Board proposed the creation of an airmobile division[1] and, to verify the concept, the 11th Air Assault Division (Test)[2] was formed at Fort Benning, Georgia, on 7 February 1963 under the command of

Notes

1 The proposed airmobile division was to comprise 14,678 men (as against a standard infantry division of 15,799) with 920 vehicles (as against to 3,671) and 400 aircraft (as against 103).

2 This designation was a tribute to the 11th Airborne Division, the 'Blue Angels', of World War 2 fame in the Pacific and an affirmation of the need for the airborne spirit within the new formation

Below: Critical to the to the overall viability of the airmobility concept was the emergence a reliable, gas-turbine powered troop transport helicopter. The Bell Model 204 was the mainstay of the US Army helicopter fleet throughout the era. More commonly known as the Huey, it was initially designated the HU-1 Iroquois in US Army service. This UH-1B is marked with a white cross for telemetry purposes during a world record attempt: it achieved a top speed of 142.2mph (the previous record by a Soviet MIL-1 was 130.8mph). (*Bell Helicopter Company*)

Above: In the heavy lift role, the 1st Air Cavalry Division (Airmobile) employed the Sikorsky CH-54 Tarhe 'Skycrane'. This CH-54A is shown lifting a complete battery of M-102 105mm howitzers – the standard artillery piece of the Air Cav in Vietnam. The M-102 was more commonly airlifted by the CH-47 Chinook. Note the rearward-facing crewman who monitors the underslung load during flight. He also controls the Skycrane's hoist during winching operations.

Brig Gen Harry W. Kinnard, together with its associated 10th Air Transport Brigade. At first it had few assets starting with only 3,000 men but gradually the army added two more brigades of infantry with artillery and support units. It was now possible to conduct battalion and brigade exercises that tested and refined the theories of the airmobility advocates.

However, there remained a dire shortage of aircraft, both rotary and fixed wing, compounded by distinct opposition from the US Air Force as the 'Skysoldiers' took to the air. While the new Bell UH-1 Iroquois helicopter provided the bulk of the lift capability and was also adaptable as an aerial weapons platform, the medium-lift Chinook helicopter was plagued with problems. Designed by Vertol and built by Boeing, the CH-47 Chinook was chronically unreliable and several were involved in catastrophic component failures resulting in fatalities. The situation became so bad that the entire airmobility test programme was put in jeopardy until improved manufacturing and maintenance procedures were instituted and the Chinook became available in acceptable numbers.

With the Chinook up and flying, it was now possible for the 11th Air Assault Division to conduct a major exercise, codenamed 'Air Assault I', involving 120 helicopters against an objective 100 miles away, the maximum range of a laden CH-47 Chinook. On 14 October 1964, despite appalling weather thanks to Hurricane Isbell offshore in the Atlantic Ocean, the helicopters struggled through the low cloud and driving rain to achieve the objective only one hour behind schedule. The exercise had been a great success and had unreservedly proved the concept of airmobility and air assault. This was confirmed in 'Air Assault II', a division-sized field exercise stretching over two states conducted in November. In the following month, the final reports were submitted to the Pentagon where many airmobility advocates believed they would languish. Furthermore, in the spring of 1965, there was a rueful expectation that the 11th Air Assault Division would be disbanded and its new-found expertise in airmobility dissipated.

The Air Assault exercises conducted during October and November coincided with the presidential elections of 1964. As the Democratic candidate, President Lyndon Baines Johnson declared that, 'American boys will not be sent to do what Asian boys ought to be doing for themselves.' Having won the election, he promptly ordered a massive escalation of American forces in Vietnam including ground troops with units of the US Marine Corps in March 1965 followed by the US Army's 173rd Airborne Brigade in May. In the same month, senior officers of the 11th Air Assault Division (Test) were closeted in heavily guarded classrooms at the Infantry School at Fort Benning to conduct top-secret map exercises. Most of the maps covered an area in Vietnam known as the Central Highlands. On 15 June, Secretary of Defense McNamara announced the creation of an airmobile division within the army force structure.

The plan called for the 11th Air Assault Division (Test) to be inactivated and its assets absorbed into an existing regular army division, which would then be converted to the airmobile role. As the existing commanding officer, Maj Gen Kinnard favoured the conversion of his former unit, the 101st Airborne Division, but the Army Chief of Staff, General Harold K. Johnson, was a former 1st Cavalry Division trooper and rank has its privileges. As the airborne divisions were part of the strategic reserve, it was felt that the ethos of the 1st Cavalry Division was more akin to airmobile operations, despite the fact that it was currently a standard infantry division based in Korea. On 29 June 1965, the colours of the 1st Cavalry Division were flown from Korea to Fort Benning. The men remained in Korea and were presented with the 'Indianhead' shoulder patch to become the 2nd Infantry Division. On 1 July, the 11th Air Assault Division (Test) stood down but was then presented with new colours to become the 1st Cavalry Division (Airmobile). At the same time, Secretary of Defense McNamara ordered the new airmobile division to be ready for overseas deployment by 28 July 1965. Overseas meant only one destination – Vietnam.

By the summer of 1965, the military situation in South Vietnam was dire with the Army of the Republic of Vietnam (ARVN) on the ropes in its war against the insurgent communist forces, known as the Viet Cong. The Mekong Delta was the main rice growing

Below: The other essential helicopter in the execution of the airmobility concept was the Boeing-Vertol CH-47 Chinook. As a medium-lift helicopter, the Chinook Ch-47A was capable of carrying up to 44 troops in the main cabin but in Vietnam the payload was much reduced because of the hot and humid conditions and a payload of 7,000lb was normal when operating in the Central Highlands. This Chinook is lifting an M-56 Scorpion tank destroyer as an underslung load.

The first real test of airmobility was undertaken by the 11th Air Assault Division (Test) during late 1964, against stiff opposition from the US Air Force. The 11th Air Assault Division (Test) became the 1st Cavalry Division (Airmobile) on 1 August 1965 and within 90 days it was in combat in South Vietnam.

area of the country and 40% of the population was situated there. They now lived under the sway of the Viet Cong with only marginal government control of the area. It was little different in the other Corps Tactical Zones (CTZ) that divided up South Vietnam. To the north of the country in ICTZ, the US Marine Corps was fighting the 1st Viet Cong Regiment in the largest American ground operation of the war so far – Operation 'Starlite'. Meanwhile, the US Air Force and US Navy had begun extensive bombing raids against North Vietnam in Operation 'Rolling Thunder' but there were few lucrative targets in an essentially agrarian society. To General William Westmoreland, the commander of MACV (Military Assistance Command Vietnam), the answer was more US troops and in particular the 1st Cavalry Division (Airmobile).

On the evening of 28 July, President Johnson announced the deployment of the division to South Vietnam. It was the first US Army division to be despatched to the country, with the Advance Liaison Detachment leaving by air on 2 August and arriving there two days later. The advance party departed between 14 and 20 August by C-124 and C-130 transport planes and landed in Vietnam with nine UH-1B helicopters and 152 tons of equipment between 19 and 27 August. They set up the division's base at An Khe, 36 miles (57km) inland from the coastal city of Qui Nhon, in the heart of IICTZ. The remainder of the division departed Fort Benning in mid-August and embarked on six troop transports, four aircraft carriers and 11 cargo ships of the Military Sea Transport Service at ports on the Atlantic and Gulf coasts. Together they carried more than 15,000 soldiers; 470 rotary and fixed-wing aircraft; 3,100 vehicles and 19,000 tons of supplies. Some of the ships sailed via the Mediterranean Sea and the Suez Canal, while the others made the western passage through the Panama Canal and across the Pacific Ocean. The long journey was largely uneventful with only the division's white mule mascot, Maggie, being inconvenienced when she was branded on the left flank by some sailors with the letters 'USN'. The time was spent undergoing further training, particularly with the new M-16 assault rifle, and preparations for jungle warfare. On 14 September, the USNS *Buckler* carrying the 2nd Brigade dropped anchor in the harbour of Qui Nhon and the first combat elements were flown directly to An Khe. Within 90 days of formal activation, the 'First Team' had been trained, equipped and transported 12,000 miles to a combat zone. The 1st Cavalry Division (Airmobile) was the first complete US Army division to be committed to the Vietnam War. The concept of airmobility and the Air Cavalry were soon to undergo trial by combat. Although the 1st Cavalry Division (Airmobile) was its official title, the formation was also known as the 'First Team'; the Air Cav; Skytroopers or Sky Soldiers; the 1st Cav and the 1st Cavalry Division during its service in Vietnam.

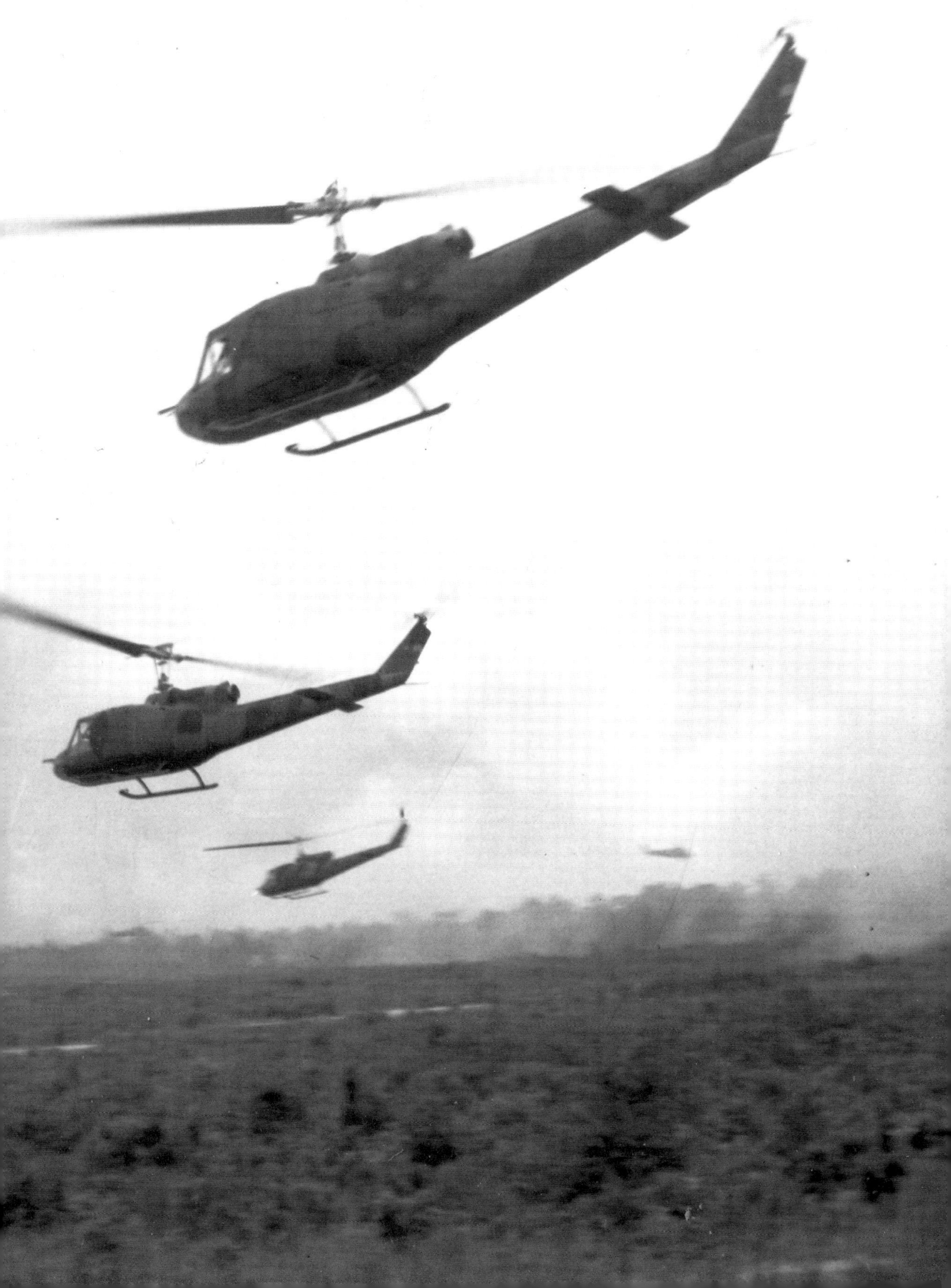

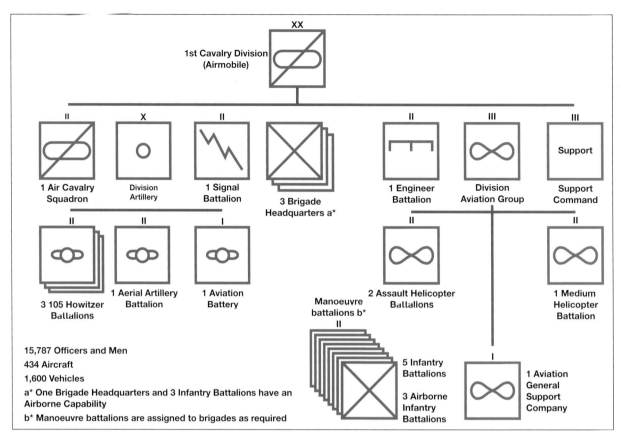

Above: Organisation of 1st Cavalry Division (Airmobile) – Summer 1965.

Below: Organisation of 1st Squadron, 9th Cavalry – Summer 1965.

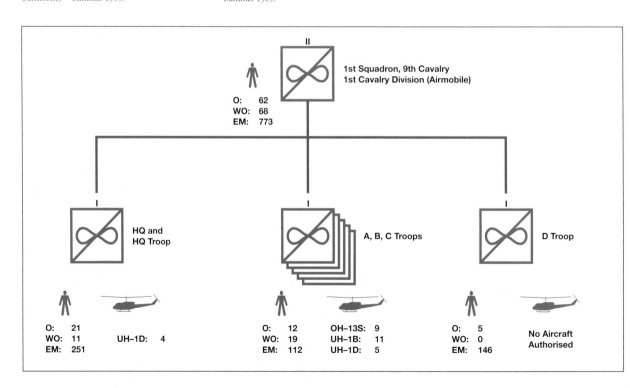

1st CAVALRY DIVISION (AIRMOBILE)
Assigned and attached units

1st Brigade
- 1st Battalion (Airborne), 8th Cavalry
- 2nd Battalion (Airborne), 8th Cavalry
- 1st Battalion (Airborne), 12th Cavalry

(Airborne capability terminated 1 Sept 1967)

2nd Brigade
- 1st Battalion, 5th Cavalry
- 2nd Battalion, 5th Cavalry
- 2nd Battalion, 12th Cavalry

3rd Brigade
- 1st Battalion, 7th Cavalry
- 2nd Battalion, 7th Cavalry
- 5th Battalion, 7th Cavalry

Division Artillery
- 2nd Battalion, 17th Artillery (105mm)
- 2nd Battalion, 19th Artillery (105mm)
- 2nd Battalion, 20th Artillery (Aerial Rocket)
- 1st Battalion, 21st Artillery (105mm)
- 1st Battalion, 30th Artillery (155mm)
- 1st Battalion, 77th Artillery (105mm)
- Battery E, 82nd Artillery (Aviation)

Division Reconnaissance
- 1st Squadron, 9th Cavalry (Air)
- 11th Pathfinder Company (Provisional)

- Company E, 52nd Infantry (Long Range Recon)
- Company H, 75th Infantry (Ranger)

Division Aviation
- 11th Aviation Group
- 227th Aviation Battalion (Assault Helicopter)
- 228th Aviation Battalion (Assault Support Helicopter)
- 229th Aviation Battalion (Assault Helicopter)
- 11th Aviation Company (General Support)
- 17th Aviation Company (Fixed Wing)
- 478th Aviation Company (Heavy Helicopter)

Division Support
- 1st Personnel Service Battalion
- 8th Engineer Battalion
- 13th Signal Battalion
- 15th Medical Battalion
- 15th Supply & Service Battalion
- 15th Administrative Company
- 15th Transportation Battalion
- 27th Maintenance Battalion
- 191st Military Intelligence Detachment
- 371st Army Security Agency Company
- 545th Military Police Company

Units temporarily attached
- 1st Battalion, 50th Infantry (Mechanized)
- 2nd Battalion, 2nd Infantry (Mechanized)
- 1st Squadron, 11th Armored Cavalry
- 2nd Squadron, 11th Armored Cavalry

The standard light observation helicopter (LOH) at the outset of the Vietnam war was the Bell OH-13 Sioux. A veteran of the Korean War when it was used primarily for front-line casualty medevac, the Sioux was replaced by the definitive LOH of the Vietnam War – the Hughes OH-6 Cayuse, more commonly known as the Loach.

IN ACTION

Right: Topographical map of South Vietnam showing the four different Corps Tactical Zones or Military Regions.

Below: Elements of the Blues – the Rifle Platoon of Troop B, 1st Squadron 9th Cavalry, known as the 'Eyes and Ears of the Division' – conduct a combat assault mission against VC and NVA troops in the An Lao Valley during Operation 'Pershing' on 28 July 1967. The antenna of the radio set makes this RTO a conspicuous target to enemy snipers; it was often shortened to reduce such exposure.

THE GOLF COURSE

While the main body of the division was on the high seas during the month-long voyage, the advance guard was busy preparing the base camp at An Khe guarded by the 1st Brigade of the 101st Airborne Division conducting Operation 'Highland'. The site chosen was a former French airstrip from the First Indochina War in the strategically important Central Highlands that form the spine of South Vietnam. There is an old Vietnamese military maxim, 'He who controls the Central Highlands controls South Vietnam'. Camp Radcliff lay astride Highway 19 and protected two vital mountain passes in an area where the Viet Minh had ambushed and defeated the French Groupement Mobile 100 just 11 years before. Anyone in control of Highway 19 had the capacity to cut South Vietnam in half: it was to be the chosen invasion route of the North Vietnamese Army (NVA) in the spring of 1975. Detritus of the battle and of the earlier French presence was all too apparent as the men cleared a new helicopter landing port under the direction of Brig Gen John M. Wright Jr, the assistant divisional commander. He decreed that heavy earth-moving equipment should not be used as this would displace the soil and create unacceptable dust clouds in the dry season and catastrophic erosion during the monsoons. Clasping a machete, Gen Wright led by example and the site was cleared of scrub by hand until, in the words of the general, 'it was as smooth as a golf course'. The name stuck and throughout the division's service in Vietnam, the helipad at the An Khe base camp was known as the Golf Course. It was surrounded by a fortified defence perimeter, some 12 miles long and 100 yards deep, called the Barrier Line.

Enemy reaction to the new camp was limited to a few light probes by some local VC guerrillas. Nervous sentries returned fire into the treeline and tragically the division suffered its first casualty in the form of the cavalry mascot, Maggie the Mule, when she was challenged and failed to impart the password. On 19 September, air and ground elements of the division supported the paratroopers of the 1st Brigade, 101st Airborne Division, during Operation 'Gibraltar'. The division was declared operational on 28 September 1965 and assumed complete responsibility for the defence of the An Khe complex. On the following day, the 1st Battalion (Airborne), 8th Cavalry, the 'Jumping Mustangs', conducted

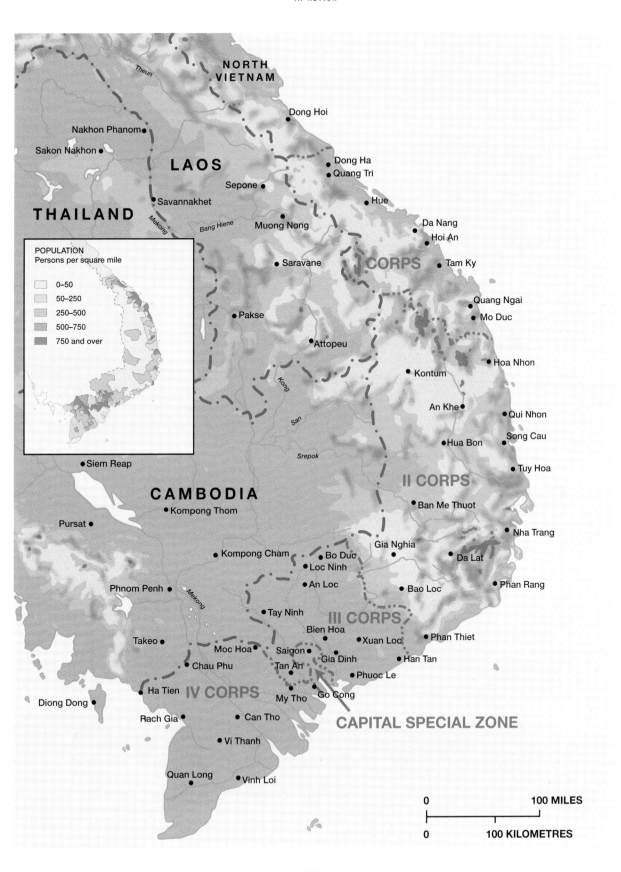

NORTH VIETNAM

Dong Hoi

LAOS

Nakhon Phanom

Sakon Nakhon

Dong Ha
Quang Tri

Sepone

THAILAND

Savannakhet

Bang Hiene

Mekong

Muong Nong

Hue

Da Nang
Hoi An

I CORPS

Tam Ky

Saravane

POPULATION
Persons per square mile

0–50

50–250

250–500

500–750

750 and over

Pakse

Quang Ngai
Mo Duc

Attopeu

Kong

Kontum

Hoa Nhon

An Khe

Qui Nhon

San

Hua Bon

Song Cau

Srepok

Tuy Hoa

Siem Reap

II CORPS

CAMBODIA

Kompong Thom

Ban Me Thuot

Pursat

Nha Trang

Gia Nghia

Kompong Cham

Bo Duc
Loc Ninh

An Loc

Da Lat

Bao Loc

Phan Rang

Phnom Penh

Mekong

Tay Ninh

III CORPS

Bien Hoa

Phan Thiet

Takeo

Moc Hoa

Xuan Loc

Saigon
Tan An

Gia Dinh

Han Tan

Chau Phu

Phuoc Le

Ha Tien

IV CORPS

My Tho

Go Cong

CAPITAL SPECIAL ZONE

Diong Dong

Rach Gia

Can Tho

Vi Thanh

Quan Long

Vinh Loi

0   100 MILES

0   100 KILOMETRES

Left: Combat troops are unloaded from USS *Boxer* on 14 September 1965 as the 15,800 men and 424 aircraft of the 1st Air Cav arrive in South Vietnam. *Boxer* carried a total of 239 aircraft comprising 57 CH-47 Chinooks, 50 UH-1 Hueys, 122 OH-13s, four CH-54 Tarhes and six OV-1 Mohawks.

Far Left: After landing at Qui Nhon, troops of 1st Air Cav disembark from a CV-2B Caribou at An Khe on 14 September 1965. The Caribou was an extremely versatile STOL utility aircraft with a remarkable rate of climb and high manoeuvrability – vital assets when trying to avoid enemy ground fire.

Below Left: An aerial view of 10 December 1965 shows the tented encampment of the living quarters and operations area at An Khe before the construction of buildings to house the command elements.

Right: Within days of the establishment of Camp Radcliff, numerous shops and bars sprang up to serve the needs of the troops and no doubt intelligence for the Viet Cong. The base camp at An Khe was named Radcliff after the division's first fatality in Vietnam.

Below: In one of the first operations by the 1st Air Cav, troops of Co A, 1/5th Cavalry, wade through a rice paddy during a sweep for the Viet Cong on 15 October 1965.

Right: The disparity in height between SFC John Lutz and his interpreter is a graphic reminder of the impact that the Americans had on their arrival. Here a peasant is questioned on the 15 October patrol.

The First of the Ninth – the 'Cav of the Cav'

The unit was formed as the air cavalry squadron of the 1st Cavalry Division (Airmobile) on 1 July 1965 drawn from equipment and personnel of 3rd Squadron, 17th Cavalry, that had been part of the 11th Air Assault Division (Test). With 62 officers, 68 warrant officers and 733 enlisted men, the air cavalry squadron comprised a Headquarters and Headquarters Troop, three air cavalry troops (Alpha, Bravo and Charlie) and a ground reconnaissance troop (Delta). Each air cavalry troop consisted of an infantry platoon known as the 'Blues' – hence Blue Platoon – transported in five UH-1D Huey 'slicks'; a White Platoon of ten OH-13 Light Observation Helicopters (LOH) that acted as reconnaissance scouts and a Red Platoon of ten Huey gunships that provided fire support to the other elements of the troop. Scout and gunship helicopters customarily flew in pairs or 'teams' for mutual support; thus two scout helicopters formed a 'White Team' and two gunships a 'Red Team'. This was the minimum for any type of operation and subsequently it was common practice to combine a scout helicopter and a gunship to become a 'Pink Team'. The Standard Operating Procedure or SOP was for the scout helicopter to fly low and slow to reconnoitre the ground while the gunship circled at altitude but ready to strike at anytime at the direction of the LOH. These initials gave rise to the term 'Loach' that usually referred to the successor to the OH-13 – the Hughes OH-6A Cayuse that was the definitive scout helicopter of the Vietnam War. Similarly the earlier gunships were superseded by the purpose-designed Huey Cobra with a much enhanced payload and performance. The combination of the Loach and Cobra made

a formidable partnership and gave rise to the 'Hunter Killer Team' with the Loach acting as the Hunter and the Cobra as the Killer. The Blues were commonly employed for ground reconnaissance, ambushes and to recover downed helicopters and rescue their crews. The Delta Troop comprised three 'Rat Patrol' platoons mounted in jeeps equipped with machine guns and recoilless rifles as well as truck-mounted mortar teams. Later in the war it was customary to absorb these assets into the Blues as the air cavalry troops proved so effective in the area war that characterised Vietnam.

It is no exaggeration to say that the helicopters of the First of the Ninth initiated over three-quarters of all contacts of the 1st Cavalry Division (Airmobile) during its service in Vietnam. The First of the Ninth – 1/9th – were the elite within an elite and an air cavalry trooper often saw more action in a month than a 'ground-pounder' did in the whole of his 365-day tour of duty in Vietnam. The air cavalry squadron was intended by the Howze Board to be the basic building block of the airmobile division. It remains intriguing that so few were actually activated when they proved so effective during the Vietnam War and none more so than the First of the Ninth – the Eyes and Ears of the Air Cav.

the first major air assault mission into the Vinh Thanh Valley supported by 16 UH-1D helicopters of the 227th Assault Helicopter Battalion. Employing the full panoply of USAF tactical air support, tube artillery, aerial rocket artillery and helicopter gunships, the battalion executed a successful landing but no enemy were encountered although 22 Skytroopers were wounded due to punji sticks: these were sharpened bamboo stakes that were capable of penetrating the jungle combat boot, being concealed as booby traps for the unwary. They were often tipped with excrement to cause infection of the wound, requiring extensive medical treatment. The 'Jumping Mustangs' had proven the concept of Combat Air Assault. On 10 October, the first brigade-sized airmobile assault was conducted with Operation 'Shiny Bayonet' involving the 1st and 2nd Battalions, 7th Cavalry, and 1st Battalion, 12th Cavalry, supported by the 1st Battalion, 21st Artillery, and the divisional air reconnaissance group – the 1st Squadron, 9th Cavalry, under the dynamic leadership of Lt Col John B. 'Bullwhip' Stockton. As so often during the war, the VC/NVA declined to join battle and only minor contacts occurred before the enemy slipped away to its sanctuaries in Cambodia and elsewhere.

THE BATTLE OF THE IA DRANG VALLEY

On arrival in Vietnam, the divisional commander, Maj Gen Harry W. Kinnard, was instructed, 'Harry, your job with your division is to prevent the enemy from cutting the country in two.' A major enemy offensive was expected in the Central Highlands with the intention of splitting South Vietnam before the build-up of American ground forces became too powerful. On 19 October, a potent force of the B-3 Front comprising the 33rd and 320th NVA regiments under the command of General Chu Huy Man, launched a concerted assault against the US Special Forces camp at Plei Me in western Pleiku province while setting ambushes for any relief forces. The offensive was also intended to lure the newly arrived American 'Sky Soldiers' into battle so as to learn their fighting techniques. The official historian of the People's Army of Vietnam, Maj Gen Hoang Phuong, was a lieutenant colonel at the time of the Ia Drang campaign and he recalls:

'When we received the news that the 1st Air Cavalry had come to Vietnam, the commanders of our divisions in the South were very nervous, very worried by what they were hearing about this strong, mobile unit so well equipped with helicopters. The liberation forces moved mainly by foot, were poorly equipped. Our hospital and food services were not good. How could we fight and win against the cavalry?…We foresaw that the coming battle would be very fierce. First, we evacuated the population and prepared training camps. We improved our positions, dug shelters, and prepared caches of food and underground hospitals. We knew sooner or later that you would attack our zones and we tried

Below: Pleiku campaign October to November 1965.

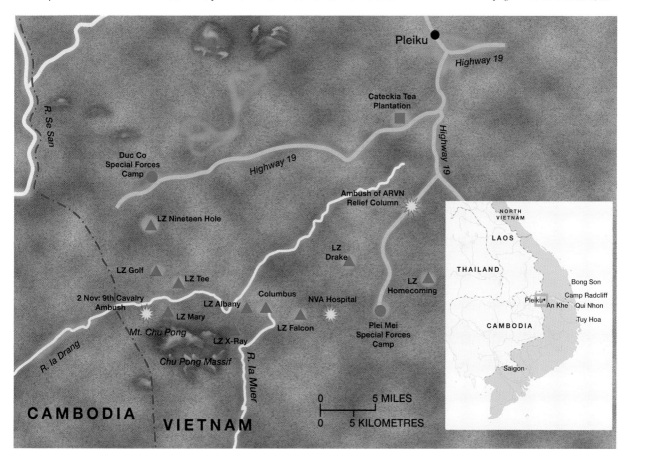

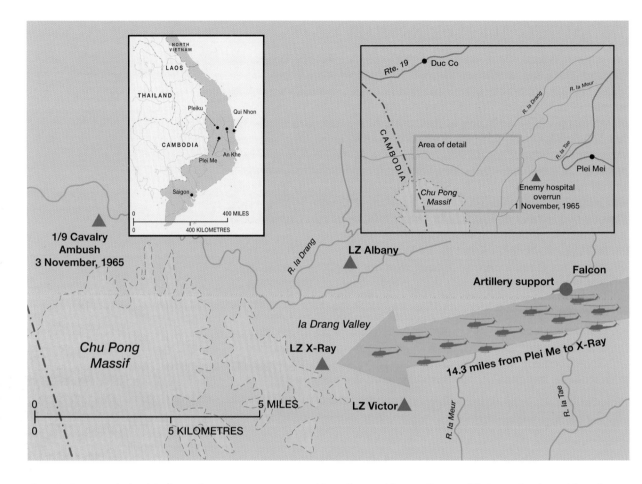

Above: Combat air assault of 1/7th Cavalry into the Ia Drang Valley, 14 November 1965.

Right and Far Right: The standard weapon carried by Huey slicks was the M-23 Armament Subsystem, Helicopter, 7.62mm Machine Gun, Door Mounted. It comprised two 7.62mm M-60D machine guns and two mounts, one on each side of the aircraft. A 500-round ammunition box was attached to the base tube assembly. Rounds were fed to the weapon by flexible chuting or else the belt was free, as shown here. A B-3 size C-ration can was usually fitted to the assault bag-fastening slide as a feed guide to reduce the likelihood of stoppages.

to prepare positions that would neutralise you. We knew that it would not be enough just to make propaganda saying that we were winning. We had to study how to fight the Americans.'

Following ferocious fighting, the attack on Plei Me was thwarted and the two NVA regiments retired to regroup at their base camp below the Chu Pong Mountain. There they met up with newly arrived 66th NVA Regiment that was near its full strength of three battalions; each of 40 officers and 513 enlisted men. The three battalions were dispersed around a large clearing near the base of the mountain.

At that time, the code letter of the 66th Regiment was X to shield its identity. On the evening of 13 November, the operations officer of 1st Battalion, 7th Cavalry, Capt 'Matt' Dillon, identified the same clearing as the landing zone for the battalion in its forthcoming operation against the NVA and gave it the codename LZ X-Ray.

Throughout their retreat from Plei Me, the 33rd and 320th NVA Regiments were pursued by the OH-13 LOHs of Lt Col 'Bullwhip' Stockton's 1/9th Cavalry, who directed the infantry battalions of the 1st Brigade into blocking positions as the enemy fled westwards. On 1 November, LOHs of 1/9th Cavalry spotted unusual activity five miles (8km) west of Plei Me camp and the squadron quickly committed its rifle platoons – the Blues – supported by its gunships – the Reds. It was soon apparent that an enemy hospital complex had been discovered and a fierce firefight developed with the NVA losing 78 KIA and 57 captured as against five troopers KIA and 17 WIA. Inserted by UH-1 helicopters, the airmobile infantry of the 1st Brigade scored some notable successes over the next few days such as the action on the night of 3 November when Blue team riflemen of Troop C, 1/9th Cavalry, ambushed an NVA heavy weapons company only to be attacked in force by the 8th Battalion of the 66th NVA Regiment. The situation was dire and only relieved by the first night-time use of aerial rocket artillery support by the gunships of the 2nd Battalion, 20th Artillery (Aerial Rocket), firing in close support. Even so the NVA continued the assault. The Blues called for reinforcements and Dustoff medical evacuation helicopters. Illuminated by a circling flareship, Company A of 1/8th Cavalry – the 'Jumping Mustangs' – made the first nocturnal helicopter combat assault in warfare soon after midnight. Together, they fought off repeated NVA attacks until the enemy withdrew as daylight dawned. Over 150 enemy casualties were inflicted at a cost of four US soldiers dead and 25 wounded.

Further fierce fighting occurred on 6 November when Company B of 2/8th Cavalry clashed with the 6th Battalion, 33rd NVA Regiment. The enemy was heavily entrenched and the attacking platoons were soon pinned down until reinforced by the battalion's Charlie Company. All the while intensive supporting fire from tube artillery and gunships pounded the enemy. But the NVA was learning quickly and moved in as close as possible to the American positions so that it became nigh on impossible to direct fire support without hitting US troops. These 'hugging' tactics were to become a familiar methodology to negate American superior firepower and were known to the NVA as 'grabbing the enemy by the belt buckle'. It was a costly firefight with 26 US dead and 53 wounded. Further sweeps around Plei Me now netted only stragglers and confirmed that the NVA had withdrawn to the Chu Pong Mountain. On 9 November, the 1st Brigade was relieved by the 3rd under the command of Col Thomas W. Brown. He was given the mission to pursue the enemy into the Ia Drang Valley. Colonel Thomas decided to commit the 1st Battalion, 7th Cavalry, commanded by Lt Col Harold 'Hal' G. Moore, into the fray. It was time for the Air Cavalry to go on the offensive.

At 1048 hours on Sunday 14 November, the first of 16 UH-ID Hueys of the 229th Assault Helicopter Battalion flared and landed among the high swaying elephant grass of Landing Zone X-Ray. The area was interspersed with anthills up to eight feet high that afforded excellent cover. Bravo Company under the command of Capt John D. Herren

secured the LZ as Company A commanded by Capt Ramon A. Nadal arrived and the perimeter expanded as Lt Col Hal Moore set up his command post. At 1120 hours, a prisoner was captured who divulged the alarming intelligence that LZ X-Ray was surrounded by no less than three enemy battalions of NVA regulars: a force of some 1,600 as against 175 air cavalry troopers dotted around the clearing beneath the Chu Pong Massif. Not surprisingly, thoughts of Little Big Horn crossed the minds of several men in the command group. As Hal Moore later recalled, 'It certainly entered my mind that we were the 7th Cavalry Regiment and by God, we couldn't let happen what happened to Custer.'

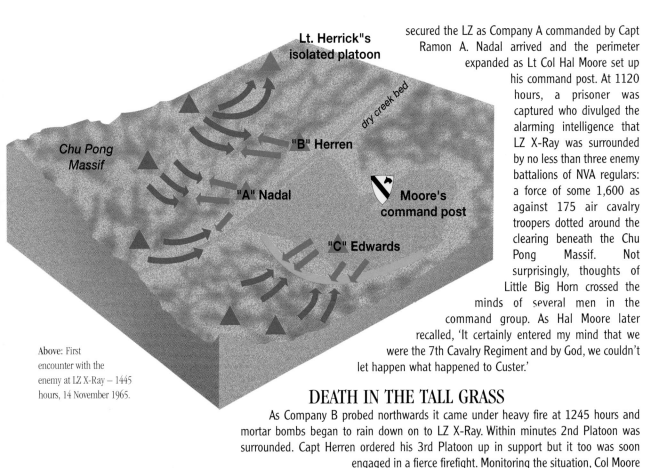

Above: First encounter with the enemy at LZ X-Ray – 1445 hours, 14 November 1965.

Below: 1/7th Cavalry fights for its life at LZ X-Ray – 0725 hours, 15 November 1965.

DEATH IN THE TALL GRASS

As Company B probed northwards it came under heavy fire at 1245 hours and mortar bombs began to rain down on to LZ X-Ray. Within minutes 2nd Platoon was surrounded. Capt Herren ordered his 3rd Platoon up in support but it too was soon engaged in a fierce firefight. Monitoring the situation, Col Moore called up air strikes and artillery support but the smoke of battle and lack of well-defined terrain features made the task of fire support co-ordination extremely difficult for the forward air controllers and artillery observers. The NVA however had excellent observation points on the Chu Pong Massif and the enemy mortar fire was now repeatedly hitting the landing zone. Several helicopters ferrying Company D were hit but none was actually shot down. Col Moore was forced to halt further helicopter landings so no more reinforcements or medical evacuation flights were possible for the time being. To the south of LZ X-Ray Company C under Capt Robert H. Edwards was staving off repeated enemy attacks. He radioed to Colonel Moore, 'We are in heavy contact. These guys are good!' The fighting was now intense but gradually the weight of fire support began to tell and enemy action slackened. Col Moore ordered Alpha and Bravo Companies to pull back to the landing zone and set up a defensive perimeter for the coming night.

During the withdrawal, the 2nd Platoon of Company B remained surrounded. A desperate counterattack was mounted to relieve the isolated men but to no avail. Many acts of gallantry occurred during the course of the attack including the action of Lt Walter J. Marm Jr who single-handed destroyed an NVA machine gun position with hand grenades resulting in the first of 25 Medals of Honor to be awarded to the 1st Air Cavalry Division (Airmobile) in Vietnam.

Meanwhile the remainder of the battalion was inserted by helicopters as well as Company B of 2nd Battalion, 7th Cavalry, that landed by 1800 hours. At the same time, 2nd Battalion, 5th Cavalry, conducted an air assault into LZ Victor some five miles southeast of LZ X-Ray with the intention reinforcing overland in the morning. During the evening, a pathfinder team was inserted to set up a night landing zone to allow reinforcement and medical evacuation of the many wounded throughout the hours of darkness.

During the night, the remnants of the surrounded 2nd Platoon of Company B suffered repeated attacks. With the platoon commander and platoon sergeant dead, the survivors were under the command of Sgt Clyde E. Savage who displayed cool and determined leadership throughout. Each assault was defeated by rifle and fire support directed by Sgt Savage. When daylight broke, the numerous bodies of enemy dead surrounded the position. The 2nd Platoon itself had suffered eight killed and 12 wounded in action. Only seven men remained unhurt. With daylight the battle was joined with renewed ferocity.

The enemy struck from the south inflicting heavy casualties on Company C of 1st Battalion, 7th Cavalry, followed by a furious assault against Company D to the east, resulting in fierce hand-to-hand combat with shovels and bayonets. Every single one of Company C's officers was either killed or wounded. With heavy fire sweeping the LZ, reinforcements arrived by helicopter and overland as the 2nd Battalion, 5th Cavalry, marched from LZ Victor. Against such odds the NVA slipped away and Col Moore ordered his depleted companies to sweep the area and search for their dead and wounded littering the perimeter. During the afternoon of 16 November, Col Moore's 1st Battalion, 7th Cavalry, was relieved and returned by helicopter to Camp Holloway near Pleiku – the battle for LZ X-Ray was over and the area was abandoned on the

Below: The last enemy attacks on LZ X-Ray – 0600 hours, 16 November 1965.

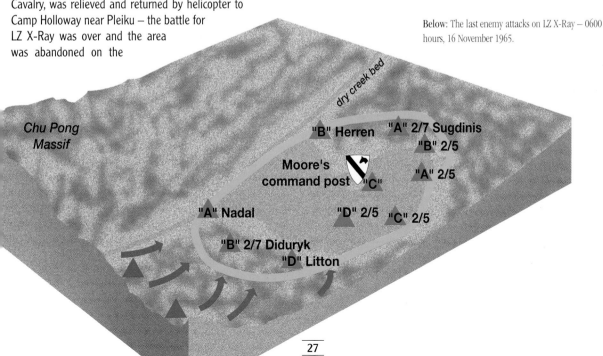

following day prior to a B-52 airstrike against the Chu Pong Massif, the first time this awesome weapon was used in the tactical support role under the codename 'Arclight'. A contemporary article in *Time* magazine[1] stated:

> 'Four days and nights the battle of X-Ray raged, while a remarkable concentration of American firepower kept the estimated two attacking NVA battalions at bay. The 1st Air Cav's artillery poured more than 8,000 rounds into the area, firing so fast that their barrels often glowed red with heat. By day and night, tactical air pounded the enemy, and for the first time, the giant B-52s from Guam were used in tactical support, blasting suspected enemy concentrations in the lowering mountains around X-Ray.'

THE AGONY OF ALBANY

The enemy lost a confirmed 834 soldiers at LZ X-Ray and an estimated 1,200 more of the 66th NVA Regiment in the immediate vicinity. American losses were 79 killed and 121 wounded but the campaign was not over yet. On the morning of 17 November, 2nd Battalion, 7th Cavalry, under the command of Lt Col Robert A. McDade Jr, with the attached Company A of the 1st Battalion, 5th Cavalry, moved out northwards to avoid the 'Arclight' strike area, scheduled for 1117 hours. The troopers marched towards a clearing codenamed LZ Albany from where they were to be extracted by helicopter. As the article in *Time* magazine said:

Below: With its characteristic single rotor blade secured, a UH-1D is recovered by a Chinook of Bravo Company, 228TH Assault Support Helicopter Battalion. The helicopters of the ``US Army during the Vietnam War period were named after native North American Indian tribes.

> 'Wednesday morning [17 November], X-Ray proudly theirs, the "First Team" split into two units and moved on. For one unit, some 500 men from the 5th and 7th Regiments, it was a move towards near disaster. Barely three miles north of X-Ray, the long column crossed the Ia Drang River. There lay two North Vietnamese soldiers sleeping in the grass, a sure sign that more trouble was not far away. It wasn't. Suddenly from all sides came a deadly hail of gunfire. The enemy seemed to be everywhere – slung in trees, dug into anthills, crouching behind bushes. It was a classic horseshoe trap, the fields of fire obviously meshed in perfect ambush.
>
> 'As the US force scattered and took cover, a Communist battalion sliced through its middle, cutting the Americans into two isolated halves. "After that," said an officer later, "it was man-to-man, hand-to-hand fighting between two very well-disciplined and very determined outfits." Though artillery and air support were soon on the way, and reinforcements were rushed from Pleiku (where many were abruptly called out of a memorial service for their dead at Chu Pong), Ia Drang quickly succeeded Chu Pong as the costliest battle of the war in human lives.'

Indeed, the battle of LZ Albany resulted in one of the highest day's casualty rates of the entire Vietnam War with 151 troopers killed and 121 wounded out of a total of some 400 men.

The Ia Drang campaign lasted some 35 days and to the US high command it was a resounding success and a total vindication of airmobility. Whole brigades were deployed successively by helicopter into otherwise inaccessible terrain to find, fix and destroy the enemy through superior firepower. The full panoply of American weapons was brought to bear against the enemy from the innovative M-16 assault rifle to the fearsome B-52 bomber. The divisional artillery fired 40,464 rounds and rockets during the campaign and the worth of the Aerial Rocket Artillery gunships was proven to the full, often firing within 165ft (50m) of American positions.

Yet the cost was high with the 1st Air Cavalry Division (Airmobile) suffering 334 dead, 726 wounded with 364 non-battle injuries and 2,828 succumbing to diseases such as malaria and scrub typhus. This represented a casualty rate of over 25% of the division's authorised strength of 15,955. Many of the sick and injured returned to service as 5,211 replacement troopers joined the division before the end of the year. NVA casualties were estimated to be some 3,561 dead out of a total force of 6,000.

This ratio of enemy dead was deemed to be unsustainable to the US high command at 11:1 as compared to US losses. Thus was born the concept of attrition and the 'body count' as an appalling measure of success on the battlefield. At the same time, despite claiming victory, the Americans left the battlefield to be reclaimed by nature. In an 'area war' or a 'war without fronts', there was no strategic imperative to seize and hold territory. It was a type of warfare that the American public found hard to understand. It was to have significant repercussions as the years went by and discontent with the conduct of the war grew at home.

After the first major encounter of the US Army and the NVA of the Vietnam War, both sides drew their own conclusions. The battle of the Ia Drang Valley was of considerable significance and set the pattern of military operations for much of the war. It was the first full division-scale air assault in military history augmented by an unprecedented level of co-ordinated fire support throughout the campaign. General Westmoreland was now a firm convert to airmobility and vertical envelopment thanks to the efficacy of the gas-turbine-powered helicopter, even in the hostile hot and humid environment of Vietnam. Combat air assaults were now to be one of the prime means to find and fix the enemy in ever larger 'search and destroy' missions. Fifty-nine helicopters were damaged by enemy fire during the campaign but only four were shot down, of which three were

Below: The withdrawal from LZ X-Ray to LZ Albany – Morning, 17 November 1965.

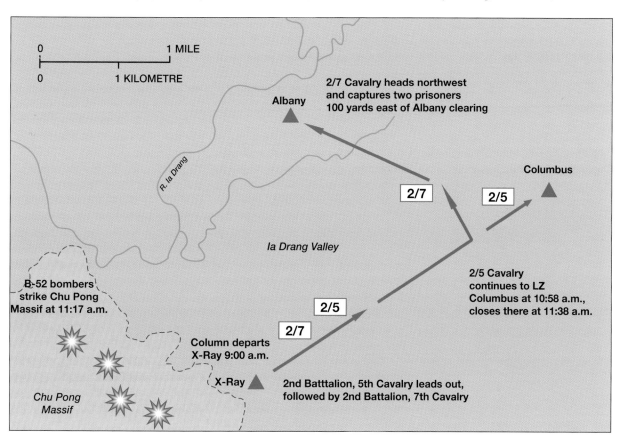

A SURVIVOR OF LZ ALBANY

Vietnam Veteran Jack P. Smith gave this speech on 8 November 2003, at the Ia Drang Survivors Banquet in Crystal City, Virginia

I have pancreatic cancer. If it is Agent Orange, it's not the first time this damned war has tried to kill me.

Let me tell you about the first time. In fact, the whole and true story of my journey home from Vietnam. But before I do, let me set the scene for you.

It is November 1965. The Ia Drang Valley. The nearest town was Pleiku, a remote Vietnamese province capital. And west of town, beyond the stilted long-huts of the Montagnards, flat scrub jungle covers the hills by the Cambodian border. A smugglers' haven, and now the infiltration route for the first North Vietnamese regulars to invade South Vietnam.

American regular infantry, the first sent to Vietnam as the war escalates, have come to this border country to hunt the People's Army of Vietnam. They are the men of the First Air Cav, the first Army infantry division to ride into war in helicopters. The leading unit is Lt Col Hal Moore's 1st Battalion, 7th Cavalry Regiment. Driving their choppers into a Landing Zone designated X-Ray, a few miles from the Cambodian border, on 14 November 1965, they land on top of a North Vietnamese Army base. A ferocious battle ensues that lasts three whole days. Hal Moore's battalion several times comes within inches of being overrun. In the end, reinforced to brigade strength, the US troops destroy the better part of a North Vietnamese division at X-Ray. Seventy-nine Americans are killed, 121 wounded, a total of 200 US casualties, the highest toll of the war till then... but there are roughly two thousand North Vietnamese casualties.

I came in on the last day of the battle. I remember the NVA bodies were piled so thick around the foxholes you could walk on them for 100 feet in some places. The American GIs were the same colour as the dirt and all had that thousand-yard stare of those newly initiated to combat.

The next day, after a restless night, my battalion, the 2/7th, walked away from X-Ray toward another clearing called LZ Albany. Around lunchtime, we were jumped by a North Vietnamese formation. Like us, about 500-strong.

The fighting was hand-to-hand. I was lying so close to a North Vietnamese machine-gunner that I simply stuck out my rifle and blew off his head. It was, I think, the only time during the war that a US battalion was ever overrun. The US casualties for this fourth day of battle: 155 killed, 121 wounded. More dead than wounded. The North Vietnamese suffered a couple of hundred casualties.

The fight at LZ Albany was largely overlooked as an aberration – poor leadership, green troops. In this first encounter between their main force regulars, the two sides focused instead on X-Ray. Interestingly, both drew the same conclusion: that each could win using the tactics of attrition.

The ferocity of the fighting during those four days was appalling. At one point in the awful afternoon at Albany, as my battalion was being cut to pieces, a small group of enemy came upon me, and thinking I had been killed (I was covered in other people's blood), proceeded to use me as a sandbag for their machine gun. I pretended to be dead. I remember the gunner had bony knees that pressed against my sides. He didn't discover I was alive because he was trembling more than I was. He was, like me, just a teenager.

The gunner began firing into the remnants of my company. My buddies began firing back with rifle grenades, M-79s, to those of you who know about them. I remember thinking, 'Oh, my God. If I stand up, the North Vietnamese will kill me; and if I stay lying down, my buddies will get me.' Before I went completely mad, a volley of grenades exploded on top of me, killing the enemy boy and injuring me.

It went on like this all day and much of the night. I was wounded twice and thought myself dead. My company [Company C] suffered about 93 percent casualties – 93 percent.

This sort of experience leaves scars. I had nightmares. For years afterwards I was sour on life, by turns angry, cynical, and alienated.

Then one day I woke up and saw the world as I believe it really is, a bright and warm place. I looked afresh at my scars and marvelled, not at the frailty of human flesh, but at the indomitable strength of the human spirit. This is the miracle of life. Like other Vietnam veterans, I began to put the personal hurt behind me, and I started to examine the war itself and to make sense of it.

When I went back to Vietnam a few years ago, I met General Vo Nguyen Giap, the man who engineered the defeat of the French at Dien Bien Phu and then commanded North Vietnamese forces in the war with South Vietnam and us. He conceded that because of the Ia Drang his plans to cut Vietnam in half and take the capital had been delayed ten years. But then, he chuckled, it didn't make a difference, did it?

We won every battle, but the North Vietnamese in the end took Saigon. What on earth had we been doing there? Was all that pain and suffering worth it, or was it just a terrible waste? This is why Vietnam veterans often have so much trouble letting go, what sets them apart from veterans of other wars...

Jack Smith died of cancer on 7 April 2004, probably due to exposure to the dioxin-based defoliant Agent Orange.

recovered. Typically, the helicopters delivered 500 tons of supplies a day and consumed 50,000 gallons of aviation fuel. Aviation units transported 5,048 tons of cargo to the troops in the field while a further 8,216 tons was despatched to Pleiku from supply depots on the coast, primarily Qui Nhon and Nha Trang.

General Westmoreland said, 'The ability of the Americans to meet and defeat the best troops the enemy could put into the field of battle was once more demonstrated beyond any possible doubt, as was the validity of the Army's airmobile concept.' But the assessment from 'the other side of the hill' was equally confident. Following the Ia Drang campaign, Senior General Vo Nguyen Giap wrote, 'After the Ia Drang battle we concluded that we could fight and win against the Cavalry troops. We learned lessons from this battle and disseminated the information to all our soldiers. These were instructions on how to organise to fight the helicopters. We thought that the Americans must have a strategy. We did. We had a strategy of people's war. You had tactics, and it takes very decisive tactics to win a strategic victory. You planned to use Cavalry tactics as your strategy to win the war. If we could defeat your tactics – your helicopters – then we could defeat your strategy. Our goal was to win the war.' In essence, Westmoreland remembered LZ X-Ray; Giap remembered Albany.

Yet the North Vietnamese plan to split South Vietnam in half had been thwarted and was not to succeed for another decade in a costly and protracted struggle. Despite suffering appalling casualties, the NVA had proved to be a formidable enemy – highly disciplined, adept at night fighting with well-rehearsed and executed assault plans and with excellent morale and esprit de corps to match that of the Sky Soldiers. Whereas the typical American unit needed tons of supplies each day, the NVA equivalent required just a few pounds of rice and *nuoc mam* (fish sauce) beyond a basic scale of ammunition and ordnance. This gave the NVA significant tactical mobility on the battlefield as against the detailed planning that was needed prior to any combat air assault by US forces. The 'hugging' tactics refined during the Ia Drang battles of closing with the Americans so as to negate the superiority of their fire support was decisive during the vicious hand-to-hand fighting at LZ Albany and was a lesson for future battles.

But Giap is somewhat disingenuous in his assessment: the crucial lesson of the battle of the Ia Drang Valley was the realisation that US forces were unable or unwilling to pursue the battered remnants of Giap's B-3 Front into Cambodia and defeat them utterly. Denied by political decree from hot pursuit of enemy units into the supposedly neutral countries of Cambodia and Laos, US forces were fatally hamstrung throughout the Vietnam War. With sanctuaries in Cambodia, Laos and their own homeland that were immune from US ground attack, NVA formations were able to rest and recuperate at their leisure and then resume the conflict at a time and place of their own choosing on the battlefields of South Vietnam. It was a decisive strategic advantage.

Postscript: For their part in the battle of the Ia Drang Valley, the Sky Soldiers of the 1st Cavalry Division (Airmobile) were awarded a Presidential Unit Citation – the first division of the Vietnam War to be so honoured. The deep blue streamer states simply: PLEIKU PROVINCE. It was another first for the 'First Team'.

Above: Fundamental to the success of airmobile operations in Vietnam was the heavy firepower and rapid response times of Huey gunships and Aerial Rocket Artillery that gave close air support to the troopers of the 1st Air Cav in virtually every contact with the enemy.

COMBAT AIR ASSAULT
'Happiness is a cold LZ' Airmobile Combat Assault

The principal purpose of helicopter-borne airmobility was to place combat rifle units and supporting troops on or within close assault distance of their tactical objectives. Furthermore, airmobile assault made it possible to deliver fresh riflemen at the decisive point in the battle zone unwearied by long ground approach marches, while maintaining

tactical cohesion irrespective of time, distance and terrain factors.

Airmobile operations in Vietnam were conceived in a reverse sequence known as 'backward planning'. Firstly, the ground tactical plan was prepared including the assault tactics to seize objectives, artillery and aerial fires to be employed, resupply, medical evacuation, and the extraction by air or other means of the manoeuvre elements at the completion of the mission. Secondly, a landing plan was devised to place the troops on the ground in the right order and location, integrated with their own fire support scheme. Next, an air movement plan was prepared to ferry troops and supplies by air to the landing zone (LZ). A loading plan was then developed to put troops and equipment on the correct aircraft in the right sequence at the designated pickup zone (PZ). Finally the staging plan ensured that all the elements of the Airmobile Task Force (AMTF) arrived at the PZ on time and in the proper condition to begin loading.

The majority of airmobile combat assaults were organised at battalion level with a command group comprising the AMTF commander (the ground commander who exercised control of all elements of the airmobile force); the air mission commander (controlling the aviation elements participating in the operation); and the fire support co-ordinators (both artillery and air force). Together, they devised the detailed plans that incorporated each other's contributions and requirements in the support of the ground commander's mission. During execution, the command group rode in a command and control (C&C) helicopter which was not normally integrated in the tactical flight formation but was free to move wherever the two commanders could best control the operation. If time and security considerations allowed, an aerial reconnaissance was carried out to determine approach and departure routes, the size and state of the landing zone and the most appropriate flight pattern.

The first important phase in the execution of an airmobile operation was the loading plan. Loading was essentially a matter of having troops and equipment organised into individual helicopter loads and waves so that helicopters could land directly beside each load, take troops and equipment aboard and take off in the minimum time. Once airborne, the AMTF assumed its flight formation. Dependent on the size of the force and, as importantly, the size and shape of the LZ, the formation most often adopted was a stepped V or a variation with 'heavy left' or right echelon, these being the most versatile and easy to control. Others included diamond and arrowhead formations. The helicopters flew at forty-five degrees to the side and rear of the lead ship. Flying as level as possible, helicopters in close formation were separated by one rotor diameter, in normal formation by two diameters, and in open formation by three. Flight routes were selected to minimise interference by enemy forces and to maintain cover and concealment.

Since it had to be assumed that the enemy was defending every landing zone, it was highly desirable that airmobile landings be made within range of supporting artillery. As a rule, all combat assault landings were preceded by preparatory artillery bombardment and airstrikes or, on occasions, by small reconnaissance parties acting as pathfinders to mark the landing zone. The security thus gained for the assault force outweighed any attendant loss of surprise. The enemy offered three main threats to airmobile assault

Above: Ho Chi Minh Trail and communist infiltration routes into South Vietnam.

Above Left: An officer and his RTO radioman monitor the arrival of a flight of UH-1D Hueys as they come in to land to pick up troops for yet another 'search and destroy' operation.

Left: Troopers of the 1st Air Cav's 3rd Brigade run from a CH-47A Chinook on LZ5 during Operation 'Masher' in February 1966. Such was the political micro-management of the war that President Johnson objected to such a bellicose term as 'Masher' so the operational name was changed to 'White Wing'.

Above: A CH-47A Chinook of the 228th Assault Support Bn prepares to lift an M-101A1 105mm howitzer of Bty B, 2nd Bn, 17th Artillery, at An Khe in March 1966. A battery of 105mm howitzers complete with a basic load of ammunition could be airlifted to a range of 100 miles in 11 Chinook sorties.

forces. First, claymore mines and improvised explosive devices were placed in the landing zone itself and in the adjacent treeline, to be detonated either electrically or by pressure on the approach of helicopters and troops.

Second, enemy personnel and weapons were located in prepared positions around the edge of the landing zone and several yards back into the surrounding vegetation.

Third, enemy forces positioned several hundred yards from the landing zone could deploy to attack the assault forces during or immediately after the landings.

Direct fire support was crucial to deal with each of these potential threats and included mortar, artillery, naval gunfire, tactical aircraft, strategic bombers and armed helicopters (the latter to be discussed later). During a specific operation the AMTF could be supported by any or all of these means which were controlled by the command group in the C&C helicopter. A combination of air strikes and artillery was used on enemy emplacements around the perimeter of the landing zone to a depth of 150-225ft (45–70m) back into the vegetation. Medium and heavy artillery was preferred because 105mm rounds were largely ineffective in destroying well-built bunkers. Similarly, bombs weighing at least 500lb (225kg) were necessary to destroy landing zone defences, while 750lb (340kg) or 1,000lb (450kg) weapons were better. Aircraft also flew runs perpendicular to the treeline, dropping napalm to splash back under the jungle canopy and into the embrasures and firing apertures of enemy bunkers. These same fires often disrupted the mines and explosive devices placed in the treeline. The deeper targets located in areas several hundred yards from the landing zone were engaged by artillery.

Air strikes and artillery had to be planned and co-ordinated so that both forms of attack were employed simultaneously and continuously. The standard and simplest method was to divide the landing zone through its centre – the fire support co-ordination line – and to assign airstrikes to one side and artillery to the other. All the while consideration had to be given to the artillery gun target lines (it was not uncommon for several artillery units to be firing on the target from more than one fire support base), and also to the direction of attack and break-away of the tactical air support aircraft, so as to prevent the helicopter formation from flying through its own artillery barrage or the flight pattern of high-performance aircraft which required considerable airspace to manoeuvre. Preparatory barrages around the landing zone were usually brief but intense, typically of five to ten minutes duration, and ended with a last WP (White Phosphorous) round to signal artillery 'tubes clear' one or two minutes prior to the troop lift transports crossing the LZ threshold. The armed helicopter gunships then made rocket and strafing runs and marked the landing points for the lead helicopters with smoke.

As the landing zone was approached, the helicopters of the AMTF moved into close formation and dropped in altitude. In most combat assaults the preferred approach was a high speed letdown (for maximum rate of descent) with a right turn into the landing zone, which allowed the flight leader to observe the LZ throughout the manoeuvre. This straight-in approach was most frequently used to effect the initial landing in the minimum space and time. A spiralling approach in formation was considered the least desirable for an assault landing because it could less effectively be supported by gunships, but was sometimes necessary, especially in hilly terrain.

During final descent further suppressive fire was delivered to the edges of the LZ by the door gunners of the troop transports. If space permitted all aircraft attempted to land simultaneously, with the lead helicopter well forward on the landing zone. Landings were effected with the minimum of hovering so as to allow each helicopter to move in as undisturbed air as possible, thus deriving maximum lift at minimum power under the existing circumstances – especially important when operating under critical load conditions. Furthermore, when landing troops, they and their equipment were less affected by rotor wash and the resulting wind-blown debris.

While on the landing zone and prior to take-off, the flight commander issued a typical radio message: 'Lift off in 15 seconds.' The other pilots were thus prepared to depart the LZ at the same time so as to reduce the possibility of fire being concentrated on a single helicopter. On take-off, the flight commander radioed, 'Lift-off, breaking right' or 'breaking left' if different from the briefing. This allowed the transport helicopters to anticipate the manoeuvre and also notified the gunships of the flight's intention. Any terrain features that might conceal enemy positions such as villages, river banks or ridge lines were avoided, whenever possible, during departure. Military power was used until a safe altitude was reached.

Below: CH-47A Chinooks of the 228th Assault Support Bn carrying members of the 1st Air Cav lift off under the covering fire support of M-114A1 155mm howitzers during Operation 'Masher' near Bong Son on 25 January 1966.

Above: In difficult terrain it was common practice to jump from a hovering Huey – often causing sprained or broken ankles. Here, troopers of the aerorifle platoon of Bravo Troop, 1/9th Cavalry, disembark from a UH-1D during Operation 'Oregon'. The trooper in the foreground has an XM-148 rifle which incorporated a grenade launcher below his M-16 assault rifle that fired 40mm grenades out to a range of 100 yards.

A typical combat air assault mission as described by Robert Sisk, formerly a warrant officer with C Company, 229th Assault Helicopter Battalion, 1st Cavalry Division (Airmobile), took place on 1 August 1966, when the 'First Team' provided support to the 3rd Brigade, 25th Infantry Division during Operation 'Paul Revere II' when it made contact with four NVA regiments. It was the 50th operation for the Air Cav since its arrival in Vietnam:

'My company, "Charlie" or C Company, 229th Assault Helicopters, was despatched to Landing Zone "Oasis", a forward firebase southwest of Pleiku. Our area of operations extended from Pleiku to the Cambodian border and included the Chu Pong Mountains and the Ia Drang Valley, all covered by thick, triple-canopy jungle. At LZ "Oasis", the first battalions of the 7th and 12th Cavalry plus units of the 2nd Battalion, 7th Cavalry, were massing for air assaults.

'During our briefings, we were told all of the landing zones would probably be "hot" and booby-trapped. The weather was exceedingly bad: torrential rains, low-lying clouds and ground fog. This was to be my first combat air assault. I was nervous and excited.

'The door gunners and crew chief made last minute checks on their machine guns and loaded belts of ammo into the gun chutes. The infantrymen were busy

writing letters and preparing for the air assaults, checking packs, cleaning weapons and hooking hand grenades to their belts.

'Several LZs were to be assaulted simultaneously. Slicks from the 227th and 229th Assault Helicopter Battalions were to air-assault the grunts into the LZs while the big Chinooks of the 228th would sling the artillery into place once the LZs were secured.

'We lifted off in flights of four. Once airborne, the helicopters joined up in a diamond formation. Chief Warrant Officer Neil Stickney was the aircraft commander, I was the co-pilot. Our flight would be the second wave into the landing zone, following four slicks from the 1st Platoon of Charlie Company. We were to maintain a one-minute spacing between formations. Behind us were two more flights of four ships each, for a total "gaggle" of 16 helicopters. On each side of the gaggle, B-model Huey gunships from Delta Company flew shotgun for the assault helicopters.

'Each helicopter was assigned a colour code with a number-small plates on each side for easy identification. This helped the infantrymen find their assigned helicopter and it also determined the position in the formation we would be flying. "Wagonwheel Six" was designated the codename for Maj Williams, who was flying the lead ship. Yellow One. He gave orders to the aircraft commanders

Above: Several experiments were conducted to allow helicopters to land in heavily wooded terrain such as this steel mesh netting laid across the treetops. It did not prove successful and it was easier to lower combat engineers who cleared an LZ using explosives and chainsaws to remove the trees and vegetation.

Far Left: Troops of the 5th Bn, 7th Cavalry look somewhat bemused as they try to knot together a 'Swiss Seat' during instruction at An Khe into rappelling – the technique that allowed a quick exit from a hovering helicopter. The nearest trooper displays the subdued divisional patch on his shoulder.

Left: With the Swiss Seat secured, a trooper begins his descent from a UH-1D Huey during an exercise conducted at An Khe on 31 January 1967.

Below Left: After their unhappy entry into service, early Chinooks underwent 1,334 separate modifications to increase flight safety. They quickly proved their worth and were an invaluable asset to the division's air mobility. This CH-47A of Co B, 228th Assault Helicopter Bn, with the divisional insignia emblazoned on its rear pylon, is fitted with a 'Jacob's Ladder' for rappelling troops.

Below: A member of Co B, 5/7th Cavalry, rappels down a 100-foot 'Jacob's Ladder' slung below a CH-47.

to have their door gunners test-fire the M-60 machine guns. From the open doors of the ships ahead, I could see short bursts of tracer rounds spewing from the guns. Stickney told our gunners to fire a burst. The rapid chatter of each weapon was reassuring.

' "Two minutes out," the flight leader said on the UHF radio. Up ahead I could see smoke and explosions in the intended landing zone. The dark smoke and bright reddish-orange flashes of the explosions stood out against the low clouds and patches of fog. An artillery battery from a distant firebase was pounding the landing zone with high-explosive rounds.

' "Last round on the way," a voice suddenly blurted over the UHF. One ship in the flight was usually assigned to monitor the artillery FM radio frequency to advise the flight leader when the barrage was ended. The last round was "Willie Peter" [white phosphorous].

'The WP burst in the centre of the clearing, a billowing cloud of thick, white smoke. "One minute out," the flight leader said. Two aerial-rocket-artillery helicopters suddenly appeared and made firing runs down both sides of the landing zone. The ARA ships broke off their rocket runs and went into a daisy-chain holding pattern, west of the LZ. The first wave of slicks touched down. I could see the door gunners raking the jungle with machine-gun fire. Soldiers spilled out both side of the choppers and crawled for the nearest cover.

'The gunships had made the initial approach with the first flight, firing machine guns and rockets. They then swung around and escorted the next flight into the LZ. One of them was fitted with an M-5 grenade launcher, and I could see it firing into the tree line. It looked like a fat kid spitting watermelon seeds.

' "White flight short final," the platoon leader of our flight said. The first flight of slicks was still holding in the LZ while more grunts exited. Timing was critical because the following flights were on final approach.

' "If they don't get the hell out of there, we'll have to make a go-around," said Stickney. Then the flight on the LZ lifted slowly and began to accelerate straight ahead and away. I locked my shoulder harness and lowered the visor on my helmet. A few weeks earlier, another assault helicopter company had lost an aircraft when the windshield was shot out. Neither pilot had his visor down; the shredded plexiglass blinded them both. The helicopter crashed, killing the crew chief.

' "We're in contact; the LZ is hot, the LZ is hot," an excited voice suddenly blurted over the FM radio. As we touched down I could see grunts lying flat behind rotting trees and giant ant hills. To the northeast of the clearing a steady stream of tracers poured from the dense tree line of the jungle.

' "We've got automatic-weapons fire east side," the same excited voice said. "We're pinned down. Wagonwheel Six, can we get those ARA ships back in here?"

' "Affirmative, Blue Fox. Do you want just the east side hit?" Wagonwheel Six asked.

' "Roger, for now. We've got a heavy machine gun in the north-east corner and small-arms fire all along the east side," replied Blue Fox.

' "White flight is up," Stickney said, meaning all of the grunts were clear of the helicopters.

' "Lifting," the platoon leader replied. All four helicopters lifted off, still in diamond formation.

'A long stream of tracers arced up at White Two, the helicopter on the right point of the diamond. "We're taking a lot of fire," the aircraft commander of White Two said in a calm, matter-of-fact voice.

' "Green and red flights, go to a staggered trail formation. We've got room in the LZ to do it. It will give you better coverage, "Wagonwheel Six said.

' "Blue Fox, this is Black Knight Six. Do you want your reserve platoon brought in?" asked the battalion commander, orbiting in the command-and-control helicopter. Normally the C&C helicopter would orbit high over the LZ. But because of the low clouds, it had to remain low-level, well off to one side of the battle.

' "If we can get that heavy gun knocked out, I think we'll be okay," Blue Fox replied.

Above: Troopers of the 1st Air Cav move warily along a river bed, constantly checking for booby traps – the cause of many casualties to US troops in Vietnam.

Above Right: Members of Co A, 2/5th Cavalry, prepare to jump from a hovering UH-1D of Co B, 227th Assault Helicopter Bn, during an operation some six miles (10km) from Quang Tri on 13 October 1968.

Right: Troops pause in a paddy field as the RTO communicates with higher HQ. Typically, the troops remain vulnerable to enemy fire from the treeline – this illustrates how the vast majority of contacts were initiated by the enemy with the intention of inflicting a few debilitating casualties. The enemy then quickly withdrew before retaliatory artillery fire and gunship support.

'"Blue Fox, this is Hog One; we're starting our run now," the ARA flight leader said. "We've got enough fuel for about two runs apiece," he added.

'"Okay, concentrate on the north-east side," said Blue Fox.

'White Flight made a left 180-degree turn and I could see the next flight of helicopters lifting from the landing zone. Streams of tracers continued to pour from the dense foliage on the east side.

'The first ARA ship was just pulling up after its rocket attack on the heavy machine gun. As the helicopter broke to the right, I saw a flash of fire from the right rocket pod. Smoke trailed from the pod and the flames were getting bigger. "We've got a pod on fire and I can't jettison it," said the pilot of Hog One. "I'm going to put down on the LZ."

'The ARA ship continued in a right turn. The last flight of slicks was just lifting off as the burning ship rolled out level and approached the landing zone. Suddenly, the flaming rocket pod exploded. The helicopter rolled violently to the left. A large piece of rotor blade broke off as the ship went inverted. Losing forward momentum, it plummeted straight down.

'"We've bought it," the pilot of Hog One said just before the ship hit the ground. It lay partially on the LZ, its broken tailboom sticking out of the heavy jungle growth. The whole aircraft was in flames. Several soldiers ran in a low crouch toward the wreckage. They were still being fired at from the tree line. "I'm going to land", said the pilot of the other ARA ship.

'"Negative; stay on station. We've got people on the ground that will get the crew out," said the battalion commander.

'"Black Knight Six, three of the crew are dead. The fourth one was thrown clear but he's hurt real bad," said Blue Fox.

'"Okay, we'll get Dust Off in there to get him out," replied Black Knight. "Also, I'm going to send your reserves in. Wagonwheel Six, pick up the ready reaction force at 'Oasis' and assault them into the same landing zone," he added.

'"Roger," said Wagonwheel Six.

'"We can't get a medevac right now; they're all busy." Black Knight said a

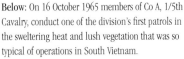

Below: On 16 October 1965 members of Co A, 1/5th Cavalry, conduct one of the division's first patrols in the sweltering heat and lush vegetation that was so typical of operations in South Vietnam.

Above: With a bottle of 'bug juice' and C-ration matches tucked into his helmet band, a squad leader points to an enemy position during a search and destroy mission conducted by the aerorifle platoon of Troop B, 1/9th Cavalry, west of Duc Pho in Quang Ngai Province during Operation 'Oregon' on 24 April 1967. Attached to the AN/PRC-25 radio of the RTO in the foreground are M-18 smoke grenades to mark friendly positions to tactical air support aircraft.

Left: A CH-47 Chinook medium-lift helicopter of the 228th Assault Helicopter Bn is loaded with ammunition crates at Camp Holloway near Pleiku that served as a forward supply point for the 1st Air Cav during Christmas 1965.

minute later. "Wheel Six, can you send one of your ships in to get that crewman out?"

' "Affirmative, sir. Green Four, break out of formation and do the medevac. Keep both gunships with you," said Wagonwheel Six.

'Green Four broke from the formation and made a left turn back into the landing zone. The two gunships continued to make firing runs on the east side of the clearing. The remaining ARA ship had knocked out the heavy machine gun and was returning to "Oasis" with its fuel critically low.

'We returned to Landing Zone "Oasis" and picked up the ready reaction force. We air-assaulted them into the same LZ, this time receiving very little ground fire.'

THE YEAR OF THE HORSE

The 1st Cavalry Division returned to its original base of operations at An Khe on Highway 19. Soon the intelligence section recommended a return to the Western Highlands early in 1966 in the hope of encountering the enemy reassembling in the unpopulated jungles. However, a new threat emerged in the Province of Binh Dinh, a region of abrupt mountains and populated coastal plains. The ARVN 22nd Division responsible for the area was spread thin as it tried to keep Highway 19 open and secure. The intelligence staff of the 1st Cavalry Division (Airmobile) confirmed that the Vietcong Main Force 2nd Regiment and 18th and 19th NVA Regiments of the 'Sao Vang' Division were operating in the area.

All the elements of a fire mission are shown in these four photographs. First (**Far Left**), the M-3 armament subsystem of a gunship of Bty A, 2nd Bn, 20th Artillery Regt, is reloaded prior to a mission.

Although the 2.75-inch FFAR (Free Flight Aerial Rocket) was deemed to be an area weapon, the pilots of 2/20th Aerial Rocket Artillery were so adept that they were able to place the 24 rockets from a pod accurately within close proximity to friendly troops to engage the enemy who commonly got as near as possible to US troops to negate the effects of fire support. As well as the rockets, the 'Hogs' were also armed with M-60D machine guns

Next (**Left**), with a 'Prick 25' on his back, an RTO of Bravo Troop, 1/9th Cavalry, directs the 'Hog' gunship to a target. (The three action photos were taken during Operation 'Pershing', a search and destroy mission in the An Lao Valley, on 28 July 1967.)

The 'Blues' of Bravo Troop take cover (**Below Left** and **Below**) as the gunship makes a firing pass at the target.

Operation 'Masher'/'White Wing' began on 25 January 1966, following the truce for the Tet holiday and Lunar New Year. These were the codenames for the operations to be launched in Binh Dinh Province by the 3rd Brigade, which began to move by road and air to staging posts in the eastern part of the province. The opening phase of the mission included 1st and 2nd Battalions, 12th Cavalry and 1st Squadron, 9th Cavalry which reconnoitred ahead of the convoy and along both sides of the road, searching for potential ambushes.

The first phase of Operation 'Masher' began on 28 January. The 3rd Brigade attacked north of Bong San from LZ Dog and quickly ran into heavy NVA resistance. However, in the first two days of February, contact with the enemy fell away as the North Vietnamese withdrew to the north and west. In the first week of combat, 1st Cavalry Division (Airmobile) lost 77 troopers while enemy losses amounted to an estimated 1,350 KIA, rendering two battalions of the 22nd NVA Regiment ineffective.

On 7 February, Operation 'White Wing' initiated the second phase of the search and destroy mission. Nine days later, on 16 February, the battle-weary 3rd Brigade returned to the division's home base of An Khe and was replaced in the field by the 1st Brigade. While 1st Brigade patrolled in the valleys around LZ Bird, the 1st and 2nd Battalions, 5th Cavalry, and 2nd Battalion, 12th Cavalry, of the 2nd Brigade encircled the Iron Triangle. With air and artillery support, the three battalions fought for four days against a tenacious enemy defence which finally collapsed after a B-52 strike.

The final phase of 'White Wing' began on 1 March with a move into the jungle-covered Cay Giep Mountains. B-52s blasted openings in the thick jungle canopy, enabling engineer teams to descend from helicopters to clear out landing zones for the 2nd Brigade. Sweeping down the slopes of the Cay Giep Mountains, the 2nd Brigade met little resistance as the main body of the NVA's 6th and 18th Battalions had pulled back immediately after the first air assault. Operation 'Masher'/'White Wing' came to an end on 6 March. By all tactical measures it was pronounced a success, having destroyed the enemy's grip on Binh Dinh Province. Once again the 1st Cavalry Division (Airmobile) had successfully combined mobility and air power. Helicopters airlifted entire infantry battalions a total of 78 times and moved artillery batteries 55 times. In 41 days of enemy

Left: A White Team of OH-6A Loaches flies low and slow, showing how dangerous the aeroscout role was when enemy groundfire could be expected at any moment. Aeroscout pilots and crew chiefs gained an uncanny sense to uncover enemy positions and then expose them to the full panoply of divisional firepower.

Below Left: A trooper is lowered into a suspected VC tunnel complex as the aerolift platoon of Bravo Troop, 1/9th Cavalry, takes part in Operation 'Oregon' on 24 April 1967.

Below: Troops search a house on 6 October 1966 during Operation 'Irving' in the area of Qui Nhon where two battalions of NVA regulars were believed to be massing for an attack on Hammond airstrip

Above: Lines of 1st Air Cav helicopters undergo maintenance on the Golf Course at the base camp at An Khe on 16 March 1966.

contact, the Air Cav engaged all three regiments of the Sao Vang Division and rendered five of its nine battalions ineffective for combat.

On 16 May, Operation 'Crazy Horse', another search and destroy mission, was launched in the jungle hills between the Suoi Ca and Vinh Thanh valleys. Initial contact was made by Company B, 2nd Battalion, 8th Cavalry and soon the entire the 1st Brigade was involved in heavy fighting with a VC regiment in tall elephant grass and heavily canopied jungle. Once the enemy was surrounded, all available firepower was concentrated on the area. The enemy regiment was hit with artillery, aerial rockets, tactical air strikes by F-4 Phantoms and bombs from high-flying B-52s. Many of its troops were cut down in ambushes as they attempted to flee the devastation and a number of important documents, detailing the Viet Cong infrastructure in Binh Dinh, were discovered.

The aim of Operation 'Paul Revere II', launched on 2 August and concluded on 15 August, was to deny areas of rich rice fields to the famished Viet Cong. Significant contact with the enemy was made on 8 August at LZ Juliett, where Company A, 1st Battalion, 7th Cavalry, came under heavy fire from a reinforced enemy battalion. In several hours of fierce fighting, Alpha Company drove off successive mass attacks. Timely artillery and air strikes prevented the enemy from surrounding the Skytroopers and the roar of helicopters arriving at LZ Juliett forced them to flee.

At the end of 'Paul Revere II', which resulted in a total of 861 enemy KIA, a task force of 2nd Battalion, 7th Cavalry, was committed to Operation 'Byrd' and despatched to Binh Thau Province, in the southern sector of II Corps, to support the Revolutionary Development Program. The heavily populated province of Binh Thau was effectively controlled by two Viet Cong battalions. The South Vietnamese government's writ ran to little more than the provincial capital, Pham Thiet, a coastal town whose economy depended on fishing and associated industries. In the previous 16 months, the 2nd Battalion, 7th Cavalry had fanned out from Phan Thiet, clearing the enemy from the populous triangle area extending to the north and west of the provincial capital and reopening the road net closed by the Viet Cong. Most significantly, the troopers reopened Highway 1, restoring the commercial link between Phan Thiet and Saigon.

One of the largest air assaults launched by the 1st Cavalry Division (Airmobile), Operation 'Thayer I', started on 13 September. Its aim was to clear Binh Dinh Province once more of NVA and VC troops and to destroy the political infrastructure of the Viet Cong. On 16 September, troops of the 1st Brigade discovered an enemy regimental hospital, a factory for making grenades, antipersonnel mines and a variety of weapons. Three days later, elements of 2nd Battalion, 8th Cavalry, exchanged fire with two NVA combat support companies.

In the opening phases of Operation 'Thayer I', elements of the 7th and 8th Battalions, 18th NVA Regiment, had been reported in the village of Hoa Hoi. The 1st Battalion, 12th Cavalry was deployed to encircle the village, and on 2 October, Company B was the first unit to be landed, some 330yd (300m) east of Hoa Hoi. It immediately came under intense small arms and mortar fire. Company A landed to the southwest to begin a move on Hoa Hoi, while Company C landed north of the village to strike south. By this time Alpha and Bravo Companies had joined up to establish positions which prevented the enemy slipping out of Hoa Hoi under cover of darkness.

During the course of the evening, Alpha and Charlie Companies of the 1st Battalion, 5th Cavalry Regiment, were airlifted into an area east of Hoa Hoi to further contain the enemy. Artillery forward observers from Battery A, 2nd Battalion, 19th Artillery, provided further assistance as enemy positions were identified and called in during the night. On the morning of 3 October, Company C, 1st Battalion, 12th Cavalry, and Company C, 1st Battalion, 5th Cavalry, attacked south to drive the remaining enemy forces towards Alpha and Bravo Companies, 1st Battalion 12th Cavalry, which were braced in strong blocking positions to receive the attack. This last action broke the enemy's resistance and the mission was completed. The pacification drive in Binh Dinh Province was stepped up with Operation 'Thayer II'. On 1 November troopers of Apache Troop, 1st Squadron, 9th Cavalry, and elements of the 5th Battalion, 7th Cavalry, were drawn into a sharp fight with Viet Cong forces in the vicinity of National Route 1 and south of the Cay Giep mountains. In Operation 'Thayer II' the enemy suffered heavy losses of 1,757 KIA.

As 1966 drew to a close, a two-day Christmas truce was observed. On 27 December, three battalions from the 22nd NVA Regiment exploited the truce to move from their usual haunts in the Hoai Nhon Delta into position for a surprise attack on LZ Bird. Three

Below: 1st Cavalry Division (Airmobile) area of operations 1965–6.

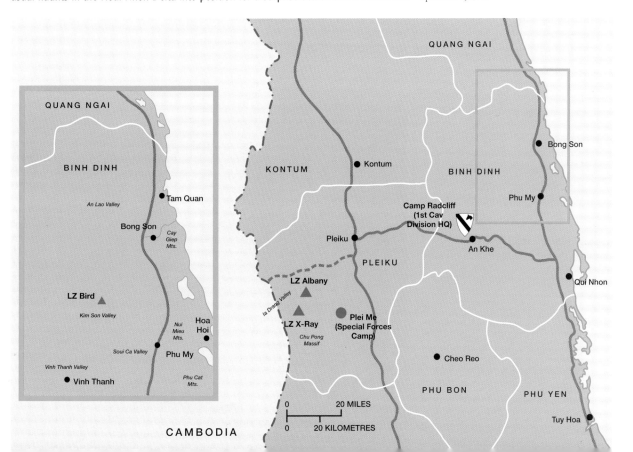

enemy units mounted a fierce infantry and mortar attack at Landing Zone Bird in the Kim Song Valley. The LZ was defended by just three understrength units: C Company, 1st Battalion, 12th Cavalry, and two artillery batteries, Battery B, 2nd Battalion, 19th Artillery and Battery B, 6th Battalion, 16th Artillery. However, the LZ was within the artillery range of two other fire support batteries. Initially, bad weather restricted air support operations and the NVA broke through the perimeter to occupy a number of gun positions. Hand-to-hand fighting ensued until some of artillery's 105mm howitzers were cranked down to pointblank range to pour 'beehive rounds into the enemy, taking a heavy toll.

For the next two days, troopers of the 1st Cavalry Division (Airmobile) pursued the fleeing NVA and made contact several times. At least 266 NVA died in this battle, in which many ARA and armed C-47 'Puff the Magic Dragon' sorties were flown. SSgt Delbert Jennings, C/2/12th Cavalry, earned the Medal of Honor for his valour in this action and went on to become the Command Sergeant Major of the 1st Cavalry Division

Below: The gun crew of the 6th Gun Section, Battery C, 1/77th Artillery, fire their M-101 105mm Light Howitzer (Towed) against VC targets in the Bong Son District during Operation 'White Wing' on 19 February 1966.

Right: One of the prime roles of the CH-47 Chinook was the creation of fire support bases to support the manoeuvre battalions in the field. The CH-47B was able to lift an M-102 105mm howitzer externally with 60 rounds of ammunition slung below and the seven-man crew carried inside the helicopter. By these means, the gun crew were ready to fire within minutes of landing while the Chinooks returned with more ammunition and ground troops to defend the newly established fire base.

in 1983. For their part in the fighting of 27 December 1966, Company C, 12th Cavalry, was awarded a Presidential Citation. Shortly afterwards the site of LZ Bird was deemed too vulnerable, and a new LZ was built on a hogback several miles to the east.

SEARCH AND DESTROY

On 13 February 1967, Operation 'Pershing' was launched in the Bong Son Plain in northern Binh Dinh Province, territory familiar to many Skytroopers. For the first time, 1st Cavalry Division committed all three of its brigades to a single battle area. ARVN troops who were familiar with Viet Cong tactics in the Bong Son Plain helped the Skytroopers to locate and eliminate the many caves and tunnels built by the enemy. For nearly a year, 1st Cavalry Division (Airmobile) scoured the Bong Son Plain, An Lo Valley and the hills of coastal II Corps Tactical Zone, seeking out enemy units and their sanctuaries. Operation 'Pershing' became a tedious and unglamorous 11-month mission which resulted in 18 major engagements and many minor skirmishes. It came to an end

Above: A battery of M-102 105mm Light Howitzers (Towed) of 2nd Bn, 19th Artillery, perches on a hilltop to provide fire support to ground troops of the 1st Air Cav during Operation 'Crazy Horse' on 15 May 1966. The M-102 weighed 3,298lb—as against 4,466lb for the earlier M-101—and was capable of firing three rounds a minute out to a range of 12,576 yards.

Above: The gun crew of an M-114A1 155mm Medium Howitzer (Towed) reposition their artillery piece at Fire Support Base Grant in October 1969. It is mounted on a 'speedjack' that allowed the rapid traverse of the weapon which weighed 12,950lb. The M-114A1 was the heaviest weapon in the Divisional Artillery so much fire support was provided by the helicopter gunships of the Aerial Rocket Artillery.

on 21 January 1968 and was the longest of the First Cav's actions in Vietnam. It accounted for 5,401 enemy soldiers killed and 2,400 captured. In addition some 1,300 individual and 137 crew weapons were destroyed.

Moving to I Corps. Vietnam's northernmost tactical zone, the division established its base at Camp Evans. On 31 January 1968, amid the celebrations of the Vietnamese New Year, the enemy launched the Tet Offensive, a major effort to overrun South Vietnam. Some 7,000 well-equipped and experienced NVA regulars blasted their way into the imperial city of Hue, overpowering all but a few pockets of resistance held by ARVN troops and US Marines. Within 24 hours, the invaders were joined by a similar number of reinforcements, while to the north of Hue five North Vietnamese and Viet Cong battalions attacked Quang Tri City, the capital of South Vietnam's northern province.

The Cavalry's immediate response was to despatch four companies of Skytroopers from the 1st Battalions of, respectively, 5th and 12th Cavalry Regiments to the village of Thorn An Thai, east of Quang Tri. Under heavy rocket attack, the enemy quickly broke off the assault on Quang Tri, split up into small groups and attempted to escape. Quang Tri was liberated within ten days.

After fierce fighting at Thorn La Chu, the 3rd Brigade moved on the embattled city of Hue. The southwest wall of the city was quickly taken after the 1st Battalion, 7th Cavalry, overcame fierce enemy resistance to link up with the 5th Battalion. By late February, the invaders were driven from Hue and the Tet Offensive was over. With some 32,000 killed and 5,800 captured, the Viet Cong and NVA had suffered a massive defeat.

After the Tet Offensive, the 1st Cavalry Division (Airmobile) embarked on Operation 'Pegasus' to relieve the 3,500 US Marines and 2,100 ARVN soldiers besieged at Khe Sanh by an enemy force of some 20,000 men. On 1 April 1968, the 3rd Brigade made a massive air assault within five miles of Khe Sanh Combat Base, followed by 1st and 2nd Brigades and three ARVN battalions. Company A, 2nd Battalion, 7th Cavalry, led the way, followed by Company C, 2nd Battalion, 7th Cavalry. After four days of hard fighting, they marched into Khe Sanh and assumed the defence of the battered base. Pursuing the retreating North Vietnamese, 1st Battalion, 12th Cavalry, recaptured the Special Forces camp at Lang Vei, uncovering large stockpiles of supplies and ammunition. In Operation 'Pegasus', 1,259 enemy soldiers were killed and more than 750 weapons were captured.

On April 19 1968, Operation 'Delaware' was launched into the cloud-shrouded A Shau Valley, near the Laotian border and 28 miles (45km) west of Hue. None of the Free World forces had been in the valley since 1966 which was now being used as a way station on the supply route known as the Ho Chi Minh Trail (see map on page 33). The first engagements were made by the 1st and 3rd Brigades. Under fire from mobile 37mm cannon and 0.50-calibre machine guns, they secured several landing zones. For the next month the brigades scoured the valley floor, clashing with enemy units and uncovering huge enemy caches of food, arms, ammunition, rockets and Russian-made tanks and bulldozers. By the time that Operation 'Delaware' was ended on 17 May, the Viet Cong sanctuary was thoroughly disrupted.

At the end of June, the 3rd Squadron, 5th Cavalry (Armored) of the 9th Infantry Division was assigned to support the Skytroopers during Operation 'Jeb Stuart III'. Operating under the tactical control of the 2nd Brigade, 1st Cavalry Division (Airmobile), it was given the mission of securing the Wunder Beach complex and the access road to Highway I, near Camp Evans in Quang Tri Province. At 0900 hours on 27 June, Troop C,

3rd Squadron, 5th Cavalry (Armored) came under rocket-propelled grenade (RPG) fire as it was undertaking a detailed search of an area known as the 'Street Without Joy'.

Anticipating the onset of heavy fighting, the inhabitants of the nearby coastal village of Binh An, began to flee the area. An NVA soldier, hiding in the column of refugees, was captured and interrogated. He revealed that the entire 814th NVA Infantry Battalion was in the village. A and B Troops of the 3rd Squadron, 5th Cavalry, along with D Troop, 1st Squadron, 9th Cavalry, closed on the village, joining C Troop, 3/5th Cavalry, and trapping the enemy within a cordon of overwhelming firepower in clear daylight and good weather conditions.

Besides Division Artillery, fire support was supplemented by Marine artillery fire from Quang Tri, Tactical Air Control (TAC) aircraft from Da Nang and the five-inch guns of a US Navy destroyer. The NVA battalion in Binah An was subjected to a seven-hour pounding. During the afternoon, Company D, 1st Battalion, 5th Cavalry and Company C, 2nd Battalion, 5th Cavalry were airlifted into an adjacent LZ and closed on the village. To deny the enemy the opportunity to infiltrate their lines under the cover of darkness, it was decided to overrun the enemy positions during the night. The guided missile cruiser, USS

Below: The ground crew rearm an AH-1G Cobra gunship with 2.75-inch FFAR and 7.62mm ammunition for the XM-28 Armament Subsystem. This weapon system comprised either two 'miniguns' or two XM-129 40mm grenade launchers or one of each.

Right: Drinking water was a precious commodity in the field and there was never enough for washing so troops took every opportunity to wash themselves and their sweaty uniforms when they encountered a river.

Below: 1Lt James Graham, the Executive Officer of Co C, 2nd Bn, 12th Cavalry, distributes mail during Operation 'Thayer I' on 19 September 1966. Mail was and will always be vital to the morale of troops in the field and it was one of most important items delivered by resupply helicopters.

Left: Aircraft maintenance was a constant task to keep the helicopter fleet of the 1st Air Cav aloft. Here, SP4 Auburn Lemon Jr repairs an ammunition linker of a UH-1C 'red ship' of B Troop, 1/9th Cavalry.

Below: Sgt George Nemosbatho, a mortar platoon squad leader of 1/12th Cavalry, takes a break with a drink of fresh coconut milk in the village of Troun Lan, Binh Dinh Province, during Operation 'Pershing' on 9 June 1967.

Average Monthly Combat Stores	
Ammunition	4,609 tons
Fuel	4,010,700 gallons
Defence stores	749 tons
Clothing and equipment	1,082 tons
Foodstuffs	1,005 tons
Rations	597,311 meals
Milk	944,780 pints
Ice cream	11,430 pints
Ice	2,777 tons

Boston, arrived at dusk and in an all-night bombardment her basic load of eight-inch shells was exhausted. It was an appalling night for the enemy troops trapped within the tight cordon. Disorganised, some of the survivors attempted individual escapes and were soon rounded up by tanks mounting searchlights and two US Navy 'Swift' patrol boats operating close to the shoreline. At 0930 hours on the following morning, a final assault was made on the enemy. In the after battle assessment, 253 of the 814th NVA Infantry Battalion were KIA and 44 were taken prisoners while the 5th Cavalry suffered only three casualties.

In late 1968, the Division moved southwards and set up operations in III Corps Tactical Zone with Divisional Headquarters at Phuoc Vinh. The Air Cav assumed a tactical area of responsibility embracing four provinces: Phuoc Long, Binh Long, Tay Ninh and Binh Duong. The beginning of 1969 found the First Cavalry Division (Airmobile) and ARVN forces engaged in Operation 'Toan Thang II'. During the first three weeks of the operation, the Skytroopers uncovered one of the largest caches of munitions found in the Vietnam War.

In February 1969, Operation 'Cheyenne Sabre' was launched with the aim of straddling and cutting enemy infiltration routes to the northeast of Bien Hoa. The rest of the summer was relative calm – until the night of 12 August when the VC unleashed simultaneous attacks against Quan Lai, LZ Becky, LZ Jon, LZ Kelly and LZ Caldwell. The VC assaults were repulsed suffering heavy losses as they fled in retreat. In the final months of 1969, the 'First Team' blocked enemy infiltration along the roads, trails and narrow paths of the Serges Jungle Highway which was hidden beneath the canopy of heavy jungle growth. The year 1969 ended on a high note for the 1st Cavalry Division: the enemy's domination of the northern areas of III Corps had been decisively smashed.

On 1 May 1970, the 'First Team' spearheaded the incursion into Cambodia striking what was previously an inviolable Communist sanctuary. Pushing through the 'Fish Hook' region of the border area, 1st Air Cav occupied the towns of Mimot and Snoul, scattering the enemy forces and depriving them of large quantities of supplies and ammunition. On 8 May, the Skytroopers of the 2nd Brigade found an enemy munitions base that they dubbed 'Rock Island East'.

Ending on 30 June, the incursion into Cambodia far exceeded all expectations and proved to be one of the most successful operations conducted by the 'First Team'. All aspects of ground and air combat elements were utilised to the full. The enemy lost enough men to field three NVA divisions and weapons to equip two. A year's supply of rice and corn was seized. The Skytroopers and ARVN forces discovered huge quantities of ammunition, including 1.5 millions small arms rounds, 200,000 anti-aircraft rounds and 143,000 rockets, mortar rounds and recoilless rifle rounds as well as 300 trucks.

The campaign had severe political repercussions in the United States for the Nixon Administration. Domestic pressure was mounting to remove America's fighting men from the war in Vietnam. Although there would be further combat assault operations, the conflict was beginning to wind down for many US Army units.

Above Right: An AH-1G Cobra gunship rolls into the attack during the incursion into Cambodia of 1970 with the terrain feature in the background marking the border with Vietnam. The narrow profile of the Cobra as compared as compared to the UH-1B/C/M models made it a more difficult target to hit and the VC/NVA showed great respect for what they termed the 'skinny helicopter'.

Right: A Red Team of AH-1G Cobra gunships resplendent with fearsome shark mouth markings conducts another fire-support mission during the incursion into Cambodia in May 1970.

VIETNAMISATION

In July 1970, the 1st Cavalry Division continued the task of clearing NVA combat elements from the region of III Corps Tactical Zone, to the north, east and west of Saigon, an immense area of approximately 4,500 square miles. In addition, the process of Vietnamisation accelerated with many Skytroopers devoted to the task of passing the bulk of the ground fighting to the ARVN forces. As other US Army units departed from

Vietnam, some of their equipment passed to the Air Cav. In particular, the First of the Ninth received a significant infusion of Loaches to augment its strength; many of these were fitted with miniguns to give them an offensive capability. In October 1970, this force was augmented by the attachment of the 3rd Squadron, 17th Cavalry, to the division, together with other elements such as the Rangers of Company H, 75th Infantry, to form a provisional Air Cavalry Combat Brigade, as had been originally been recommended by the Howze Board.

Above: A CH-47A Chinook of Co B, 228th Assault Support Helicopter Bn, comes to the hover to pick up another slung load of 105mm ammunition for the guns of 2/19th Artillery firing in support of ground elements of the 1st Air Cav during Operation 'Thayer I' on 28 September 1966.

The 9th Air Cavalry Brigade (Combat) was officially authorised on 5 December 1970 with the mission of supporting ARVN units on an area basis. In February, the brigade supported an ARVN operation in Cambodia but the Vietnamese lacked the flexibility and military skills to conduct swift moving airmobile combat assaults. Accordingly, with no American troops fighting on the ground, the brigade never realised its full potentiality and it was gradually allowed to wither on the vine.

Although 26 March 1971 officially marked the end of operations in Vietnam for the 1st Cavalry Division (Airmobile), President Nixon's programme of Vietnamisation required the continued presence of a strong US fighting force. The 2/5th Cavalry, 1/7th Cavalry, 2/8th Cavalry and 1/12th Cavalry along with specialised support units such as Troop F, 9th Cavalry, and Delta Company, 229th Assault Helicopter Battalion remained in Vietnam to become the 3rd Brigade, 1st Cavalry Division (Separate) with its headquarters at Bien Hoa and an assigned strength of 7,632 men. Subsequently known as Task Force Garry Owen, its primary mission was to interdict enemy infiltration and supply routes in War Zone D, encompassing some 3,500 square miles. On 5 May 1971, the colours of the 1st Cavalry Division (Airmobile), except those of the 3rd Brigade, were furled in Vietnam and flown to Fort Hood, Texas. Meanwhile, the 3rd Brigade (Separate) was now defending the Saigon/Long Binh US military complex and acting as a regional ready reaction force.

On 1 April 1972, the North Vietnamese Army began a major offensive across the DMZ and from the Fishhook area of Cambodia. By 3 April, these thrusts became a full-scale attack. More than 48,000 NVA troops hit Loc Ninh. Two days later, on 5 April, the North Vietnamese threw heavy assaults against An Loc and the brigade's air assets were heavily involved in containing the onslaught. In April and May, massive bombing missions by B-52s blunted the North Vietnamese invasion. Large groups of enemy soldiers were caught in the open fields and entire NVA units were destroyed. Helicopters and gunships from the 3rd Brigade saw heavy action at An Loc and Loc Ninh, engaging tanks as well as ground troops.

On 15 May, relief units advanced down Highway 13 and broke through to help lift the bitter siege of An Loc. The NVA was reeling after suffering huge losses and began to withdraw to sanctuaries in Cambodia and Laos. The 1972 Easter offensive aimed at cutting South Vietnam in half had failed. The helicopter air effort of the 3rd Brigade had turned in a magnificent performance in support of the remaining advisors with the ARVN units. During the period from 5 April through to 15 May 1972, numerous T-54 tanks, armoured personnel carriers and anti-aircraft guns were knocked out in the area around An Loc.

In June 1972, the stand-down ceremony for the 3rd Brigade (Separate) was held in Bein Hoa and its colours were returned to the United States. The last Skytrooper left Tan Son Nhut Airbase on 21 June, completing the division withdrawal that had started on 5 May 1971. With the departure of the 3rd Brigade, the 1st Cavalry Division (Airmobile) had been the first US Army division to be deployed to Vietnam and was the last to leave.

Above: Purple Haze – a radioman of Bravo Troop, 1/9th Cavalry, sets off a smoke grenade to mark a pick up zone for a Huey to extract his aerorifle team after an operation. The blue scarf was an obvious unofficial item worn by the 'Blues' of the 1/9th.

Right: Sgt William Patterson, the squad leader of 1st Pl, Co D, 1/8th Cavalry, and SP4 Hugh Shipp, an artillery FOO, search a well in the village of Mi Duc on 9 August 1967. Note the standard yellow divisional patch worn at this date while the soldier on the right has the subdued patch on his left shoulder but the full colour insignia of the 82nd Airborne Division on his right, indicating an earlier combat tour. In the background is an M-42A1 'Duster' twin 40mm anti-aircraft gun used in the ground-support role.

INSIGNIA, CLOTHING & EQUIPMENT

Above: Being 10in shorter and 1.5lb lighter than the M-16, the XM-177E2 or Colt Commando was favoured by specialised troops such as this K-9 dog handler with his German Shepherd preparing to move out on an operation.

UNIFORMS

Trooper, 1st Cavalry Division (Airmobile), 1970 (right)

The US armed forces in Vietnam were well equipped for jungle warfare with improvements in weapons and clothing being introduced throughout the conflict. Beside his personal weapon, the most important item was the Tropical Combat Uniform as worn by this Air Cavalry Trooper depicted during the Cambodian incursion of 1970. From top to bottom, he wears an M-1 helmet with reversible camouflage cover although by this stage of the war individual additions such as beads and a 'peace medallion' were commonplace to accompany the cigarette pack and insect-repellent 'bug juice' bottle in the helmet band. Around his neck is the chinstrap of his soft 'boonie hat' that sits atop his heavily laden rucksack. This type is the nylon Tropical Rucksack that was based on the ARVN model with an X-frame but of larger dimensions with a third external pocket. It was introduced for US troops in late 1968. The rucksack has attachment points for other pieces of equipment including a one-quart water canteen and the Lightweight Entrenching Tool in its M-1967 nylon carrier. Tucked into the top flap of the rucksack is a 66mm M-72 Light Anti-Tank Weapon or LAW. This one-shot disposable weapon was highly effective against enemy bunker systems. The Tropical Rucksack is suspended from the M-1967 Modernized Load Carrying Equipment or MLCE that was essentially identical to the previous M-1956 web gear but with nylon substituted for canvas and plastic for metal fittings. These allowed quicker drying and were unaffected by the mildew prevalent in Vietnam. Here, two M-1967 ammunition

From top to bottom: First, a 1st Air Cav badge with hanger manufactured by the Vietnamese and sold to the Skytroopers in the shops around camp. Next a cavalry flash; third, a belt buckle also manufactured locally by the Vietnamese.

pouches as well as two M-26 fragmentation grenades are attached to the web equipment belt fitted with a quick-release 'Davis' buckle. Below his belt is a cotton bandolier holding seven 20-round M-16 ammunition magazines, although experienced soldiers invariably loaded only 18 or 19 rounds into each clip to minimise the risk of jamming. In his right hand is an M-1942 machete and in his left an XM-177 or CAR-15 (Colt Automatic Rifle). This was a shorter and lighter version of the M-16 assault rifle. On the left shoulder of the tropical coat is the subdued sleeve insignia of the 1st Cavalry Division (Airmobile). The trouser cargo pockets are typically full of gear and are bound around the lower leg with bootlaces to prevent snagging on foliage. The tropical combat boots are the improved 1966 version with the 'Panama' pattern tread to prevent the build-up of mud between the cleats and with a spike-resistant insole to defeat punji sticks.

Pilot, 227th Aviation Battalion (Assault Helicopter), 1970 (right)

The integral aviation assets and their personnel were the key to the success of the 1st Cavalry Division (Airmobile) in Vietnam. There was a constant shortage of pilots and aircrew to serve the thousands of aircraft in Southeast Asia. At the height of US involvement, in March 1970, there were 3,926 US Army helicopters in South Vietnam. As early as January 1966, lack of aviators was threatening the entire viability of airmobility in Vietnam. Officer pilots were withdrawn from US Army and US Marine Corps formations across the world for service in Vietnam and veterans of the conflict were returned on further tours of duty with increasing regularity. Helicopter qualification courses were shortened but, even so, by June 1966 there were still only 9,700 pilots as against an Army requirement of 14,300. By now, the US Army's aviation school at Fort Rucker was working at full pitch to produce as many officer pilots as possible for immediate deployment to Vietnam. As in World War 2, the solution to the problem lay in allowing other ranks to become aviators, drawing on a generation of young and daring warrant officers that proved to be ideally suited to flying in the dangerous and demanding environment of South East Asia alongside commissioned pilots. Between 1961 and 1973, a total of 1,045 Army aviators was killed on flying duties in Vietnam. The most common type of aviation unit was the Assault Helicopter Company or AHC. When not flying, the most common form of headgear was the baseball utility cap obtained locally in theatre complete with embroidered captain's bars and aviator's wings. Introduced in 1969, the Shirt and Trousers, Flying, Hot Weather Fire Resistant was manufactured from 4.4oz Nomex synthetic material. The shirt featured two chest pockets and a pen pocket on the upper left sleeve. The trousers had two large thigh pockets for maps and both the wrists and ankles incorporated Velcro fastenings to enhance fire resistance. All flight crews were advised to avoid any form of nylon clothing as such garments could melt into the flesh in the event of fire. Accordingly, flight personnel were instructed to fly with their sleeves rolled down and hands protected by Nomex flying gloves. Similarly, tropical combat boots were eschewed as they were reinforced with nylon. Instead, most crewmen wore leather boots for increased fire protection. Subdued rank and branch collar insignia are worn on the shirt as are US Army and name tapes as well as the wings of an Army aviator. On the upper left arm is the oversize Shoulder Sleeve Insignia in US Subdued Twill of the 1st Cavalry Division (Airmobile). On the right chest pocket is the unit insignia of Company B, 227th Aviation Battalion (Assault Helicopter). The cowboy-style leather belt and holster for the .45-inch automatic pistol is a typical affectation of aviation personnel. This Vietnamese-made example features bullet loops on the belt, a twin magazine pouch at the rear and an additional one on the holster itself.

Far Left: An Air Cav trooper braces himself against the rotor downwash of a UH-1H as it takes off from an LZ northeast of Fire Support Base Gladiator during May 1971.

Above Left: With the Ranger flash and divisional patch prominent on his shoulder, Capt William E. Taylor communicates by radio to the C&C helicopter circling overhead. The standard radio for ground troops was the PRC-25, known to troops as the 'Prick 25'.

Left: Crew chief SP4 James M. Ralph refuels his UH-1D of Co A, 229th Helicopter Assault

Bn, on 14 March 1966. The helicopters of the helicopter assault battalions came under the centralised control of the 11th Aviation Group within the 1st Air Cav.

Above: PFC Roger D. Goon of Co A, 2nd Bn, 12th Cavalry Regt, takes a swig of water during a patrol from Camp Evans in January 1968. The Air Cav often carried less equipment and ammunition than standard line infantry as they could rely on rapid resupply by their own helicopter units. Even so, this rifleman carries a belt of 7.62mm ammunition for the squad M-60 machine gun.

DUST OFF – AEROMEDICAL EVACUATION

Although the helicopter was used extensively during the Korean War, the Vietnam War will forever be remembered as the helicopter war and the single machine that epitomised that more than any other was the Bell Iroquois UH-1. This remarkable aircraft was the first helicopter to be produced in large numbers that featured a gas-turbine engine. This compact and efficient powerplant was the technological breakthrough that allowed the helicopter to come of age. Design of the new helicopter began in 1955 under the designation H-40 which became the HU-1 or Helicopter Utility from which the nickname of Huey derived. The first flight of the new aircraft powered by a Lycoming T-53 engine took place in October 1956. Although classified as a utility helicopter, one of the main design parameters was for the helicopter to be able to accommodate four standard stretchers across the width of the hull for the aeromedical evacuation role. In previous designs, patients were carried in external pods that afforded little protection from the elements and did not allow any medical attention to be administered beyond a plasma drip bottle. The Bell Model 204 provided sufficient space for the stretchers as well as a medical corpsman to provide in flight emergency treatment besides the two pilots and crewchief. Production of the UH-1, as it was finally designated by the US Army, began in 1959 with the first model delivered on 30 June 1959. In its standard configuration, the UH-1A was capable of lifting two crewmen and seven passengers.

The first Huey helicopters were deployed to Vietnam in April 1962 with the arrival of the 57th Medical Detachment (Helicopter Ambulance) comprising five UH-1A helicopters in support of the 8th Field Hospital at Nha Trang. These were replaced by five UH-1Bs in March 1963 with flights spread across South Vietnam. Shortly afterwards, the 57th adopted the radio call sign 'Dust Off' that has become synonymous with aeromedical evacuation units ever since. On its arrival in September 1965, the 1st Cavalry Division (Airmobile) incorporated an air ambulance platoon. As part of the division's 15th Medical

Below: Wounded troopers of Company C, 2nd Bn, 8th Cavalry, are evacuated by a UH-1D Huey of the Air Ambulance Platoon, callsign 'Medevac', 15th Medical Bn on 5 November 1965 at the outset of the Pleiku Campaign.

Battalion, this comprised 12 UH-1D Hueys with a medical evacuation section of eight helicopters and a crash rescue section of four. Three of the latter were equipped with Kaman 'Sputnik' fire-suppression systems to enable firefighters to enter burning aircraft. However, the extra equipment so overloaded the firefighting Hueys in the hot and humid conditions of Vietnam that the system had to be abandoned and the helicopters reverted to standard helicopter ambulances.

The platoon adopted the call sign 'Medevac' and was soon heavily involved in the battle of the Ia Drang valley. With casualties averaging between 70 and 80 wounded a day, the 'Medevac' helicopters were hard pressed to meet such a commitment and, on occasions, troop lift Hueys were employed to carry the less seriously injured from the fireswept landing zones. In the first three months of operations the platoon lost two pilots killed,[1] one flight crewman wounded and nine Hueys hit by enemy fire with one shot down and destroyed on 10 October.

The fundamental purpose of the helicopter ambulance was to bring the combat casualty from the battlefield to the operating table in the shortest possible time. The seriously injured were taken directly from the field to a base hospital, often bypassing the battalion aid and clearing stations.

Dustoff crews flew some of the most hazardous combat missions of the war in their unarmed helicopters. Medical evacuation missions were received either at the divisional base at An Khe, at a stand-by area close to a particular formation conducting an operation or even in flight. Precise information had to be given to the 'Medevac' crew to effect evacuation such as co-ordinates of location, nature and number of casualties and the tactical security of the Pickup Zone. Casualties were either classified as 'urgent', 'priority' or 'routine'. 'Urgent' demanded immediate response from any helicopter ambulance in order to save life or limb, while 'priority' were those casualties who had serious but not critical wounds and were likely to remain stable for up to four hours. In practice many casualties were understandably overclassified as 'urgent'. Similarly, the security of the Pickup Zone was often exaggerated by ground units anxious to evacuate their casualties.

Once the casualties were loaded aboard, the medical corpsman identified the most serious patient, applied first aid as appropriate and reported the nature of his wounds to the aircraft commander. He in turn radioed the local medical regulating officer, who advised him of the nearest hospital with the necessary surgical capability to deal with the condition. Since most pickups were made within range of a surgical, field or evacuation

Above: Hanging on to the helicopter hoist, the crewchief of a UH-1H ambulance guides his pilot into a jungle clearing to effect an medevac.

Notes
1 Captain Charles F. Kane Jr. on 12 October 1965 and WO George W. Rice on 18 December 1965. Both were killed by single shots to the head while loading casualties in contested LZs prompting the fitting of extra armour protection to the pilots' seats of the air ambulance UH-1Ds. An additional 28 members of the Air Ambulance Platoon were killed during the Vietnam War undertaking aeromedical evacuation missions in support of the 1st Cavalry Division (Airmobile).

Above: The aeromedical evacuation helicopters of the 'Dustoff' units were a significant morale booster to the troops fighting a protracted and frustrating war against a determined enemy that rarely stood and fought except at times and places of his own choosing and when he enjoyed a local tactical advantage. Too often, troopers were injured by devious and devastating booby traps resulting in dreadful blast injuries. Whatever the cause, the casualty was assured that a dustoff helicopter would arrive as soon as humanly possible and fly him directly to hospital.

hospital, the air ambulance often flew directly to whatever facility offered the best medical care. Although the less seriously injured were sometimes evacuated too far back, the practice saved the lives of the critically wounded who required immediate life-saving surgery. By these means some 97.5% of the wounded who were airlifted from the combat zone survived their wounds. On average, the elapsed time between being injured and surgery was an hour and 40 minutes as compared to ten hours during World War 2. More than 900,000 US and allied sick and injured were evacuated between 1964 and 1973. Helicopters on aeromedical evacuation missions were three times more likely to be shot down than on all other types of flights combined. Almost a third of the 1,400 pilots that flew dustoff missions in Vietnam were killed or wounded due to hostile fire or accidents. The courage and fortitude of the 'Medevac' flight crews made an immeasurable contribution to troop morale as every trooper knew that if he was wounded he would soon be picked up by an air ambulance whatever the conditions.

DISTRIBUTION OF HELICOPTERS

The 428 authorised helicopters of the 1st Air Cavalry Division (Airmobile) were distributed as follows:

- The three infantry brigades each had eight LOHs and two UH-1Bs.
- The Air Cavalry Squadron had 30 LOHs, 38 UH-1B gunships and 20 UH-1Ds.
- Division Artillery had 12 LOHs and 43 UH-1Bs, including 36 rocket-firing Hueys and three UH-1Bs in the ARA battalion.
- The Aviation Group comprised two Aviation Battalions (Assault Helicopter). Each battalion had three LOHs and was divided into three lift companies of 20 UH-1Ds each and an armed helicopter company of 12 UH-1B gunships.
- The Aviation Battalion (Assault Support Helicopter) had 48 CH-47 Chinooks divided into three companies with 16 in each and three LOHs.
- The General Support Company had 16 UH-1Ds and 10 LOHs.
- The Support Command incorporated the Medical Battalion with 12 UH-1Ds and the two Maintenance Battalions had eight LOHs and eight UH-1Ds between them.
- From 1967, the OH-13 LOHs were replaced by OH-6A Loaches and, from 1968, the UH-1B/C gunships were superseded by AH-1G Cobra attack helicopters. All UH-1D Hueys were progressively replaced by the improved 'Hotel' model. During 1966, helicopter availability averaged 68% for Hueys, 63% for Skycranes and 43% for Chinooks reflecting the harsh operating conditions in Vietnam.

Below: UH-1D 'slicks' of the 229th Assault Helicopter Battalion lift off after inserting troopers of the 1st Air Cav. The term 'slick' was given to troop lift helicopters as distinct from the gunships that were festooned with gun and rocket pods giving rise to a host of other nicknames such as 'Hogs'.

Left: A UH-1D of Co B, 229th Assault Helicopter Bn, lifts off after dropping off supplies for Co A, 1st Bn, 7th Cavalry, during Operation 'Pershing' on 27 May 1967.

Opposite, Above: The Hughes OH-6A Cayuse was the most successful light observation helicopter of the Vietnam War. Named the Cayuse, the OH-6A was commonly known as the Loach. In White Teams of two, the Loaches scoured the countryside at low level searching for any signs of the enemy. In the 1st Air Cav, Loaches served with the 1st Sqn, 9th Cavalry, and initiated most of the division's contacts with the enemy.

Opposite, Below: UH-1D Hueys of Bravo Troop, 1/9th Cavalry, flare as they land to pick up members of the 'Blues' from the aerorifle platoon during Operation 'Pershing' on 28 May 1967, some 30 miles (50km) northeast of the divisional base camp at An Khe.

Below: A CH-54A 'Skycrane' of the 478th Aviation Co lowers a badly damaged CH-47 on to the Golf Course. The drogue parachute attached to the Chinook stabilised the underslung load in flight and prevented it from rotating. During the war, the Skycrane retrieved hundreds of aircraft valued at over $200 million.

Above: Sgt Edward A. Shelby sets the fuse of a 106mm recoilless rifle 'Beehive' round held by SP4 Melvin R. Munoz on 31 January 1967. The XM-581 anti-personnel round contained thousands of 'flechettes', small 2¼-inch arrow-like projectiles, that spread out on firing to create a devastating cone of steel against troops in the open. On Boxing Day 1966, the 22nd NVA Regiment attacked Firebase Bird held by some 100 1st Air Cav troops protecting two artillery batteries. The position was almost overrun by the NVA when the defenders responded with 'Beehive' rounds that slaughtered the attackers in their tracks. Although the Air Cav suffered significant casualties, the NVA lost 266 KIA and Firebase Bird was saved from destruction.

Right: A classic image of a Huey door gunner in action as crew chief SP4 James M. Ralph of Co A, 229th Assault Helicopter Bn, engages the enemy with his M-60D machine gun during a combat air assault on 16 March 1966.

Right: The principal weapon of the OH-6A Loach was the M-27 Armament Subsystem comprising an M-134 GAU-2B/A 7.62mm minigun with a phenomenal rate of fire – either 2,000 or 4,000 rounds per minute with an effective range of 1,000 yards. 2,000 rounds of ammunition were commonly carried inside the helicopter.

Below: An 81mm mortar crew engages the enemy in support of a 1st Air Cav operation in the Bong Son District on 19 February 1966. The 'Eighty One' was the standard infantry mortar throughout the Vietnam War and was integral to every infantry company. With a range of up to three miles, it was an area weapon with a rapid fire capability of 25 rounds a minute.

M-16 versus AK-47

The 1st Air Cav was the first major US Army formation to be equipped with the M-16 assault rifle. Indeed, the weapon was so new that much of the initial training with the rifle took place on the ships sailing for Vietnam. The M-16 was designed by Eugene Stoner of the Armalite Corporation. In 1954, the company was asked to produce a survival rifle for pilots of the US Air Force who were shot down – to kill small game for food rather than defending themselves against attack. Although the AR-5 (Armalite Five) proved perfectly effective, the USAF did not procure it in quantity although it was adopted by Special Forces units for clandestine operations in .22in Long Rifle calibre. Stoner continued development of his innovative lightweight designs combined with the advent of the 5.56mm (.223in) Fireball cartridge resulting in the Armalite AR-15. The first customer to buy the new rifle in quantity was the

British Army followed by the US Air Force in 1961 as the M-16. Two years later the US Army chose the design as its new standard infantry rifle. Production was undertaken by the Colt Firearms Company and the M-16 entered widespread service with the US Army in 1965 although Special Forces units in SE Asia procured the new weapon earlier. During acceptance trials, the M-16 proved to be highly accurate and reliable with formidable wound ballistics. The weapon proved so efficient that troops were told that it was unnecessary even to clean it. With its black plastic furniture, the M-16 was significantly lighter than its 7.62mm predecessor, the M-14, and more ammunition could be carried for the same basic load. However, once in combat in Vietnam alarming faults arose. The M-16 often suffered stoppages and jamming in combat resulting in the deaths of combat infantrymen. This provoked a scandal in Congress

and a subsequent investigation soon discovered the root cause. During trials, the 5.56mm cartridge used was commercial ammunition with a propellant known as IMR or Improved Military Rifle. Once full-scale manufacture began, a different propellant known as ball powder was used that caused a sticky residue after firing that on cooling could cause the bolt head to jam solid. A modification programme was quickly implemented together with a cleaning kit for the troops in the field and the resulting weapon was designated the M-16A1. Thereafter it gave satisfactory service for the remainder of the Vietnam War.

Calibre: 5.56mm (.223in)
Length: 990mm (38.98in)
Weight: 3.64kg (8.02lb)
Magazine: 20 or 30-round box
Cyclic rate of fire: 700 rpm
Muzzle velocity: 1,000m (3,280ft) /sec

Conversely, the weapon of choice of the Viet Cong and the North Vietnamese Army suffered no such difficulties in the field. The legendary AK-47 assault rifle, named after its inventor Mikail Kalashnikov, has proved to be one of the most widespread and successful personal weapons in military history. Much of the design is borrowed from the German Sturmgewehr 44 assault rifle and the 7.92mm kurz (short) round of World War 2. Easy to mass-produce with few moving parts for maximum reliability,

the AK-47 is a rugged and robust weapon that can absorb much hard use with the minimum of maintenance and training by the operator. Accordingly, it was the ideal rifle for a guerrilla army in the hostile environment of Vietnam where weapons had frequently to be secreted underground or even underwater for long periods. Although the Viet Cong were often equipped with the 7.62mm SKS rifle or captured French and American weapons, the NVA used both the AK-47 and the Chinese

derivative, the Type 56, in huge numbers. Firing the 7.62mm x 39 cartridge, the round combines high lethality and hitting power at the typical combat ranges encountered in Vietnam of under 300yd (275m), frequently less than 100 (90m).

Calibre: 7.62mm (0.3in)
Length: 869mm (34.21in)
Weight: 5.13kg (11.31lb)
Magazine: 30-round box
Cyclic rate of fire: 600rpm
Muzzle velocity: 710m (2,330ft) /sec

Above Right: A member of Co B, 5/7th Cavalry, demonstrates the telescopic stock of the CAR-15 or XM-177E2 version of the M-16 assault rifle. Popular with Special Forces – hence its name of Colt Commando – the CAR-15 was rarely issued to line infantry in Vietnam except for elite units such as the 1st Air Cav. Despite being more compact inside helicopters, the CAR-15 provided no great advantage over the standard M-16 to Sky Soldiers and it was not adopted in quantity.

Right: Rock and Roll – a trooper fires his M-16 assault rifle which has an XM-148 grenade launcher mounted underneath. This is an early model of the rifle/grenade launcher combination which was subsequently standardised as the M-203.

RPG-7 versus LAW

Although the VC/NVA were highly adept in their use of mortars and free-flight rockets, their principal infantry support weapons were the 75mm recoilless rifle and the RPG-7 rocket launcher. The 75mm recoilless rifle was mounted on a two-wheel carriage to provide a more stable and, therefore, more accurate firing platform. Because of its distinctive backblast, mortar sights were often attached to the weapon to allow indirect fire against US positions and firebases up to a maximum range of 2,000yd (1,830m). Although designed as an anti-tank weapon and derived from the German Panzerfaust of World War 2, the RPG-2 and RPG-7 were also used in the indirect role as surrogate artillery pieces. In the direct role, the RPG-7 fired a five-pound B-41 fin-stabilised rocket with an accurate range of 500yd (460m) and an area capability out to 1,000yd (920m). Both weapons were capable of knocking out APCs and bunkers and were also highly effective against helicopters, many of which were lost to RPGs. Tank and APC crews quickly learned to counter the RPG by erecting chain-link fencing as 'RPG Screens' around their vehicles when stationary to disrupt the warhead prior to its striking the AFV. No such measures could be taken to protect a hovering helicopter or one on short finals into a hot LZ.

At the outset, the Americans had no equivalent to the RPG although some units still used the old M-20 3.5in Bazooka and the M-79 40mm grenade launcher fulfilled part of the same role. Accordingly, the M-72 Light Anti-armour Weapon or LAW was developed. The 66mm warhead was housed in a telescopic tube housing that was extended prior to firing. As the launcher was opened, simple flip-up sights appeared and the trigger mechanism was primed. Once the rocket had been fired at the target, the launcher was discarded and another LAW was primed to continue the action. Weighing just 5.5lb (2.5kg), the LAW was accurate out to 300yd (275m) and capable of penetrating 6in (152mm) of armour or destroying a bunker system. In comparison, the RPG-7 weighed 18.7lb (8.5kg) with its attached 4.4lb (2kg) warhead. The principal difference was that the RPG could be reloaded whereas the LAW was a one-shot disposable weapon but then US forces in Vietnam could call on heavier firepower when necessary as this account by an Air Cav trooper affirms.

Private Mark M. Smith of 1st Battalion, 5th Cavalry served with the 1st Cavalry Division (Airmobile) between February 1967 and February 1968 and was on an operation in Binh Dinh Province.

'On patrol in August, my platoon found a dud butterfly bomb and determined to blow it up in place. We spent 20 frustrating minutes without managing to set it off, using hand grenades – pull the pin and run like hell for cover – and well aimed shots with M-79s. Finally one of the grenadiers, who had fired at it five or six times was fed up and snapped. "Fuck the motherfucker – call a B-52 strike in on it! 'That was always the solution – wipe things out. Run into an enemy scout, call in the gunships; meet an enemy patrol, send for the fighter-bombers; take a burst of sniper fire, radio the howitzers.

'When I achieved a position of real responsibility in Nam, platoon sergeant and platoon leader, I always told the new guys as they came to the field: "Forget everything they taught you except how to use your weapons, and follow your squad leaders." What this indicated, of course, is not that the training was that awful but that in actual combat nothing goes according to the book. Everything is hellishly confused, you can't remember hand and arm signals, you haven't the time to yell out formations, so you just yell, "Let's go, let's go! This way, let's go!" and hope your people come along.'

Nevertheless, in a typical firefight, the weapons of an infantry squad from NVA or Viet Cong Main Force units were on a par with their American counterparts

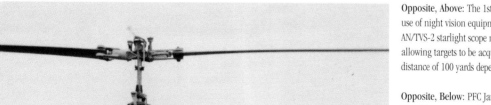

Opposite, Above: The 1st Air Cav were pioneers in the use of night vision equipment. This soldier has an AN/TVS-2 starlight scope mounted on his M-16 – allowing targets to be acquired at night out to a distance of 100 yards depending on weather.

Opposite, Below: PFC James Darwin checks out the M-134 'minigun' on the M-21 Armament Subsystem of a 'Gunfighter' UH-1B of the aeroweapons platoon, Bravo Troop, 1/9th Cavalry prior to a mission. The M-21 comprised a combination of a 'minigun' and an M-158 seven-tube 2.75-inch rocket pod.

Left: A UH-1B of the 'Red Scorpions', the aeroweapons platoon of Apache Troop, 1/9th Cavalry, completes hot refuelling during an operation on 28 May 1968.

PEOPLE

Above: General Hamilton H. Howze.

GENERAL HAMILTON H. HOWZE

Hamilton Hawkins Howze was born in West Point, New York, on 21 December 1908. The son of Maj Gen Robert L. Howze (who served under Theodore Roosevelt and his 'Rough Riders'), he attended the US Military Academy at West Point and graduated in the class of 1930, commissioned in the Cavalry.

Howze saw action in numerous European campaigns during World War 2. He earned his Army Aviator wings in 1955. He is recognised as the intellectual force behind the concept of airmobility and current Army Aviation doctrine.

While serving as the first Director of Army Aviation, Department of the Army, from 1955 to 1958, he developed new tactical principles for the employment of Army Aviation, and was instrumental in helping the Aviation Center and School become fully established in its new home at Fort Rucker, Alabama.

As Chairman of the Tactical Mobility Requirements Board in 1961, he cited the need for the development of airmobile theory and doctrine. The army's adoption of the Howze Board recommendations revolutionised mobile warfare concepts based on the use of organic aviation in much the same manner as the introduction of the tank affected mobility concepts almost 50 years earlier.

The 11th Air Assault Division (Test) was formed in 1963 to test and validate these concepts. As a result of his leadership, foresight, and perception, two airmobile divisions were eventually established in the army force structure. These divisions successfully provided the full spectrum of mobile, combined arms capabilities which are requisite to successful ground combat and which have become fundamental to modern airmobility doctrine. Later, General (then Lt Gen) Howze served as the Commander of the XVIII Airborne Corps. His last assignment was as Commander-in-Chief, US Forces Korea.

LT GEN JOHN L. TOLSON III

Colonel (later Lt Gen) John J. Tolson became actively involved with Army Aviation in 1953 while serving as Chief, Doctrine and Combat Developments, G3, Headquarters, Department of the Army. At that time he initiated the first study dealing with the tactical application of Air Cavalry. From this assignment, he moved to Fort Benning, where he was the Director, Airborne-Army Aviation Department, Infantry School, from 1955 to 1956.

During his tenure, he completed the development of initial aviation doctrine and subsequently published the first field manual governing the tactical employment of Army Transport Aviation on the battlefield. This work was validated in Vietnam and remains a basic reference for the tactical employment of Army Aviation.

In 1957, Tolson completed Fixed & Rotary Wing Qualification at Fort Rucker, and subsequently served for two years as the Assistant Commandant of the Aviation School. This was a very formative period in the School, particularly in the developing of armed helicopter concepts and the formation of the provisional air cavalry unit, the 7292nd Aerial Combat Reconnaissance Company (Provisional).

Studies by the School's Combat Developments Office produced concepts for the Air Cavalry Division. Also, lasting innovations in pilot and mechanic training were initiated during this period. From 1959 until 1961 Col Tolson served as Deputy Director of Army Aviation. It was during this period that he participated in key decisions in consolidating the family of Army aircraft for future development which later became the workhorses of the Vietnam Conflict. From April 1967 to July 1968 he served as Commanding General, 1st Cavalry Division (Airmobile), Vietnam. General Tolson subsequently became Deputy Commanding General, Continental Army Command.

Above: Lt Gen John L. Tolson III.

LT GEN HARRY W. KINNARD

Lt Gen Harry Kinnard was born in Texas and graduated from West Point in 1939. He joined the 101st Airborne Division and was the G-3 Operations Officer to Brig Gen Tony McAuliffe at the siege of Bastogne during the Battle of the Bulge. It was Kinnard who suggested that Gen McAuliffe should respond to the German demand for surrender with the single word — 'Nuts'. Kinnard became a full colonel at the age of 29 and was a seasoned authority in airborne operations before he became an Army Aviator in 1962. In the following year, he was appointed as the commanding officer of the 11th Air Assault Division (Test) to explore the concept of airmobility. Under his expert guidance, he established the feasibility of airmobility during exercises against his former unit — the 82nd Airborne Division. Using many of the assets of the 11th Air Assault Division (Test), he formed the 1st Cavalry Division (Airmobile) and within 90 days took this radically new formation into combat. Under his leadership, highly innovative techniques and ideas, such as aerial rocket artillery and night vision equipment, were refined and used to devastating effect against the enemy in Vietnam. During his year of command, the 1st Cavalry Division (Airmobile) proved its worth repeatedly and he sought to extend airmobility doctrine in his subsequent appointment as Commander US Army Combat Development Command. Ironically, Kinnard had displayed the merits of airmobility to General William Westmoreland in Vietnam but the latter was now the Chief of Staff and seemed to forget the lessons of the past. Westmoreland ordered the 1st Air Cavalry (Division) to become a Triple Capability or TRICAP division, a configuration that proved unworkable and the 'First Team's' experience as the exemplar of airmobility was lost.

Below: Lt Gen Harry W. Kinnard.

COL HAROLD G. MOORE

The word 'hero' is a much debased term through overuse and inappropriate application but for Col Hal Moore it is utterly appropriate. Born on 13 February 1922, Moore was not academically gifted and his time at West Point was a constant trial except on the rifle range where he proved to be an outstanding marksman with the M-1 rifle. After graduation in 1945, he joined the 187th Airborne Regiment and then tested parachutes at Fort Bragg, North Carolina, where on his first jump, his parachute got caught in the tailplane of a C-46 and he was dragged behind the plane at 110mph at a height of

Above: Colonel Harold G. Moore.

Right: Lt Col John 'Bullwhip' Stockton.

1,500ft (460m) until he cut himself free and deployed his reserve. From June 1952, he served in the Korean War and saw heavy action at Pork Chop Hill and elsewhere. After a posting to the Pentagon in the Air Mobility Division, he was personally chosen by Brig Gen Kinnard to serve as a battalion commander in the 1st Cavalry Division (Airmobile). He was given Col George Custer's old command of the 1st Battalion, 7th Cavalry with whom he won undying fame during the battle of the Ia Drang Valley. As the first Skytrooper to place a foot on LZ X-Ray, he was also the last to leave. He was soon promoted to full colonel and took command of the 3rd Brigade of the 1st Cavalry Division (Airmobile). He subsequently commanded the 7th Division and ended his military career as Deputy Chief of Staff Personnel, retiring in 1977 after 32 years of service. Despite his undistinguished tenure at West Point, Hal Moore was the first in his class to achieve one, two, and three stars. He was a true warrior.

LT COL JOHN B. STOCKTON

Lt Col John 'Bullwhip' Stockton was one of the outstanding cavalrymen of the Vietnam War and as such commanded the elite First of the Ninth on the deployment of the 1st Cavalry Division (Airmobile) to South Vietnam. Previously, as the commander of 3/17th Cavalry at Fort Benning in Georgia, Stockton adopted the Stetson hat based on the 1876 pattern campaign hat as the 'Cav hat' to instil esprit de corps in his troops. In addition, he favoured colourful silk cravats – the 'Cav scarf' – and decreed that his officers carry their orders in cavalry saddlebags. All these affectations were carried over to the 1st Cavalry Division (Airmobile) when the 3/17th Cavalry became 1/9th Cavalry and they subsequently spread throughout the air cavalry units in Vietnam. Through his brilliant leadership, the First of the Ninth became the premier air cavalry squadron of the Vietnam War (see separate box) and Stockton was the inspiration for the character of Colonel Kilgore played by Robert Duvall in the movie *Apocalypse Now*.

COMMANDING GENERALS VIETNAM		COMMAND SERGEANTS MAJOR VIETNAM	
Commander	**Date**	**Sergeant Major**	**Date**
Maj Gen Harry W. O. Kinnard	July 1965–May 1966	CSM Chester R. Westervelt	July 1965–June 1966
Maj Gen John Norton	May 1966–Mar 1967	CSM Kenneth W. Cooper	June 1966–June 1967
Maj Gen John J. Tolson	Mar 1967–Aug 1968	CSM William O. Marshall	June 1967–May 1968
Brig Gen Richard L. Irby	Aug 1968–Aug 1968	CSM Jack B. Moore	May 1968–Oct 1968
Maj Gen George T. Forsythe	Aug 1968–Apr 1969	CSM Vern O. Peters	Oct 1968–Dec 1969
Maj Gen E. B. Roberts	May 1969–May 1970	CSM Lawrence E. Kennedy	Jan 1970–May 1971
Maj Gen George W. Casey	May 1970–July 1970	CSM Arnold E. Orr	May 1971–Jan 1972
Maj Gen George W. Putnam	Aug 1970–May 1971	CSM William Corn	Jan 1972–July 1973
Maj Gen James C. Smith	May 1971–Jan 1973		
Maj Gen Robert M. Shoemaker	Jan 1973–Feb 1975		

MEDAL OF HONOR RECIPIENTS VIETNAM

Capt Ed W. Freeman	A Co, 229th Assault Bn	14 November 1965
2Lt Walter J. Marm	A Co, 1/7th Cavalry Reg	14 November 1965
SSgt Jimmy G. Stewart	B Co, 1-12th Cavalry Reg	18 May 1966
Sgt David C. Dolby	B Co, 1/8th Cavalry Reg	21 May 1966
PFC Billy L. Lauffer	C Co, 2/5th Cavalry Reg	21 September 1966
PFC Lewis Albanese	B Co, 5/7th Cavalry Reg	1 December 1966
SSgt Delbert O. Jennings	C Co, 1/12th Cavalry Reg	27 December 1966
PFC James H. Monroe	C Co, 1/8th Cavalry Reg	16 February 1967
Sp5 Charles C. Hagemeister	A Co, 1/5th Cavalry Reg	20 March 1967
Sp4 George A. Ingalls	A Co, 2/5th Cavalry Reg	16 April 1967
Sp5 Edgar L. McWethy, Jr.	B Co, 1/5th Cavalry Reg	21 June 1967
Sp4 Carmel B. Harvey, Jr	B Co, 1/5th Cavalry Reg	21 June 1967
Sgt Allen J. Lynch	D Co, 1/12th Cavalry Reg	15 December 1967
Sgt William D. Port	C Co, 5/7th Cavalry Reg	12 January 1968
CW2 Frederick E. Ferguson	C Co, 227th Aviation Bn	31 January 1968
Capt James M. Sprayberry	D Co, 5/7th Cavalry Reg	25 April 1968
1Lt Douglas B. Fournet	B Co, 1/7th Cavalry Reg	4 May 1968
Sp4 Hector Santiago Colon	B Co, 5/7th Cavalry Reg	28 June 1968
Sgt John N. Holcomb	D Co, 2/7th Cavalry Reg	3 December 1968
SP4 Donald R. Johnston	D Co, 1/8th Cavalry Reg	21 March 1969
1Lt Robert L. Poxon	B Trp, 1/9th Cavalry Reg	2 June 1969
Sgt Rodney J. Evans	D Co, 1/12th Cavalry Reg	18 July 1969
Sgt Donald S. Skidgel	D Co, 1/9th Cavalry Reg	14 September 1969
2Lt Robert R. Leisy	B Co, 1/8th Cavalry Reg	2 December 1969
Sp4 John P. Baca	D Co, 1/12th Cavalry Reg	10 February 1970
Sgt Peter C. Lemon	E Co, 2/8th Cavalry Reg	1 April 1970
Capt Jon E. Swanson	B Trp, 1/9th Cavalry Reg	26 February 1971

ASSESSMENT

Right: Cav Country – Principal battle areas of 1st Cavalry Division (Airmobile) from 1965 to 1971.

Most of the original units of the 1st Cavalry Division were raised in the 19th century for service in the Indian wars where they fought possibly the finest light cavalry since the Golden Horde. Whether through superior firepower or starvation, they prevailed in the harshest circumstances and a tradition of fortitude was born. In the Vietnam War, the troopers of the 1st Cavalry Division (Airmobile) fought possibly the finest light infantry of the 20th century, usually on battlefields of the enemy's own choosing. Again they prevailed, although at a high cost in men and matériel. Even though many observers dismissed and despised these respective foes as savages or racially inferior 'gooks', they were redoubtable opponents and highly skilful soldiers. It is a testament to the troopers of the 1st Cavalry Division (Airmobile) that they succeeded so often and so comprehensively against such committed antagonists. The latter's martial skills had been honed over years of warfare whereas the average trooper did his 365 days and then went home: hopefully whole in mind and body. To the trooper in a Huey or a foxhole, the Viet Cong or North Vietnamese Army soldier was a formidable fighter and worthy of respect. Although subsumed in an odious communist regime, the VC/NVA fought for a nationalist cause by the creed of their enlistment 'Death or Victory'. The 'First Team' ensured that for many it was the former and that the latter only came at an awful price.

It is one of tragedies of the Vietnam War that to the political establishment and the military high command that there was no real measure of success on the battlefield other than the repugnant 'body count' that gave an utterly unreliable kill ratio of the enemy to American dead. It is not surprising that the American public could neither understand nor support such a pusillanimous strategy as the war dragged on without resolution. Nevertheless, what was totally unacceptable was the treatment meted out to many soldiers on their return from Vietnam. Ignored by government and vilified by fellow citizens in turn, they deserved better. They had followed the demands of their country to fight in a distant alien land for a culture and cause they did not understand but they did their duty. Many paid the ultimate sacrifice with their lives and more were cruelly mutilated and scarred. As the first complete division into Vietnam and the last to leave, the 1st Cavalry Division (Airmobile) endured 82 months of combat. During that time, over 150,000 troops served with the division. They suffered a total of 32,036 killed or wounded – 5,444 KIA; 26,592 WIA. That is half as many again as the combined casualties of World War 2 (4,055) and the Korean War (16,498). The Air Cav was the only US division to fight in all four Corps Tactical Zones. It also took part in the invasion of Cambodia in 1970.

Vietnam was no minor brushfire war and Johnson's strategy of 'guns and butter' without committing the Reserves or National Guard was deeply flawed. The regular US Army and Marine Corps were bled to death in the quagmire of Vietnam to be replaced by an inadequately trained and poorly led band of draftees with no corporate experience.

NORTH VIETNAM

THAILAND

LAOS

CAMBODIA

Theun

Nakhon Phanom

Sakon Nakhon

Savannakhet

Mekong

Bang Hiene

Mun

Warin Chamrap

Pakse

Streng

Kong

Srepok

Siem Reap

Kompong Thom

Pursat

Phnom Penh

Mekong

Takeo

Diong Dong

Dong Hoi

PEGASUS: Apr 1968

JEB STUART: Jan-Mar 1968

DELAWARE: Apr-May 1968

CAMP EVANS

WHEELER/WALLOWA: Oct 1967-Jan 1968

PERSHING: Feb 1967-Feb 1968

KONTUM: 1967

MASHER/WHITE WING: Jan-Mar 1966

IRVING: Oct 1966

THAYER I, II: Sept 1966-Feb 1967

MATADOR: Jan 1966

DAVY CROCKETT: May 1966

PAUL REVERE II, III, IV: Aug-Dec 1966

PLEIKU CAMPAIGN: Oct-Nov 1965

CAMP RADCLIFF

NVA EASTER OFFENSIVE: Apr 1972

LINCOLN HOUSE: Mar-Apr 1966

NATHAN HALE: Jun-Jul 1966

HENRY CLAY: Jul 1966

CAMBODIA: May 1970

PHUOC LONG: Nov 1969

BINH LONG: Jul-Aug 1969

WAR ZONE C: 1968-1969

CAMP GORVAD

BYRD: Jul 1966-Jan 1967

WAR ZONE D: 1968-1969

NAV CAV: 1968-1969

0   100 MILES

0   100 KILOMETRES

Above: When a Loach was combined with the gunships of a 'Red Team', it became a 'Pink Team' but later in the war it became known as a 'Hunter-Killer Team' with the Loach flying low while the gunships remained at altitude ready to sweep down on any targets directed by the Loach. The 'Blue Max' insignia on the 'doghouse' of these AH-1G Cobras identifies the 2/20th Aerial Rocket Artillery that supported the 1st Air Cav throughout the Vietnam War.

It has been said that the US Army did not fight in Vietnam for eight years but eight separate armies each fought for one year or 365 days: that magic number before DEROS and a return to 'The World'. It is all the more remarkable that some formations maintained their combat effectiveness and discipline to the end. Army units such as the 'Herd', the 173rd Airborne Brigade, and the 'First Team', the 1st Cavalry Division (Airmobile), displayed commendable professionalism with much less of the indiscipline, racial tension and accusations of atrocities that bedevilled some other formations. During its service in Vietnam, the division was awarded 27 Medals of Honor; 120 Distinguished Service Crosses; 2,766 Silver Stars; 2,697 Distinguished Flying Crosses; 8,408 Bronze Stars for Valor, 2,910 Air Medals for Valor and 5,328 Army Commendation Medals for Valor.

The concept of air mobility was conceived in an earlier Asian war. It came to fruition with the arrival the 1st Air Cavalry (Division) Airmobile in Vietnam in 1965 and in the words of the divisional history, *Memoirs First Team*, air mobility was fundamental to the success of Air Cav operations during the war: 'Perhaps this is the one message that comes across louder and clearer than all others. From the Ia Drang to the A Shau to War Zone C, the 1st Air Cav, successfully and repeatedly, changed its tactics and techniques to meet the challenges of terrain, weather and the enemy.

'It is this very adaptability – this inherent propensity for doing precisely the right thing at the right time by a finely-tuned combination of men and machines – that was has made the First Team a consistent winner.

'It has been said that the Pleiku Campaign was the triumph of the airmobile concept. In truth, every battle, every campaign, every year, has been the triumph of the concept.'

Left: The opposition – the Viet Cong with their Russian-supplied AK-47s and other munitions – proved tough opponents.

Below: The Bell Huey was the workhorse of airmobility operations in Vietnam flying hundreds of sorties a day. Here, troopers of Charlie Company of 2/8th Cavalry of 3rd Brigade (Separate) load supplies on to a Huey UH-1H during the final months of 1st Air Cav operations in the Vietnam War.

Far Left: A skytrooper of 1st Air Cav whose helmet shows he is a short-timer – he's counting off the days before DEROS: Date Eligible for Return from Overseas. Photo taken during Operation 'Pershing' in 1967.

Left: The majority of helicopter losses during the Vietnam War was due to flying accidents and mechanical failure. This Huey of the 11th Aviation Company (General Support) crashed on takeoff at the Golf Course at An Khe on 5 May 1967.

Below: A spectacular method of creating an instant LZ was by dropping a 10,000lb (4,500kg) M-121 bomb with an extended fuse to detonate it above ground level for maximum blast effect and minimum cratering – here a CH-54A of 478th Aviation Co carries an M-121.

Bottom: Blues of the Aerorifle Platoon of Bravo Troop, 1/9th Cavalry, disembark from their 'Blue Lift' UH-1H during a snatch operation on 13 October 1968.

POSTWAR

RETURN TO CONUS AND REORGANISATION

Despite its success during the Vietnam War, the future of the division in its airmobile configuration remained uncertain in early 1971. The former divisional commander, Lt Gen Harry Kinnard was now the head of the Army Combat Developments Command and he wished to expand the capabilities of airmobility with further testing of the Air Cavalry Combat Brigade as first espoused by the Howze Board. However, General William Westmoreland was now the Chief of Staff and, despite being won over to the concept of airmobility in Vietnam, he decreed otherwise. The division was now converted to a 'triple capability' or TRICAP formation comprising armour, airmobile and cavalry brigades that were essentially ground based. Now based at Fort Hood in Texas, the colours of the 1st Cavalry Division (TRICAP), minus those of the 3rd Brigade (Special) still in Vietnam, were transferred to the commander of the former 1st Armored Division under the command of Maj Gen James C. Smith. The division consisted of the 1st Armored Brigade, the 2nd Air Cavalry Combat Brigade and the 4th Airmobile Infantry Brigade as well as Division Artillery and Support Command.

Field trials of the new divisional configuration were held at Fort Hood beginning in February 1972. The purpose was to investigate the effectiveness of the TRICAP concept at company and battalion level in a European mid-intensity warfare environment. By the end of June 1972, the last of the units of the 3rd Brigade (Separate) had returned from Vietnam and several famous battalions and squadrons were inactivated. The Vietnam War was over for the 1st Cavalry Division (Airmobile). The evaluation of the TRICAP concept continued until 21 February 1975 when the 1st Cavalry Division was reorganised and reconfigured as an armoured division. During 1977, it evaluated the concept of the future 'heavy division' with additional support units.

In 1979, the 2nd Blackjack Brigade of the 1st Cavalry Division deployed to Europe by sea to undertake a major NATO Reforger or REturn of FORces to GERmany exercise in the defence of Western Europe against a Soviet invasion. In the following year, the same brigade conducted Operation 'Desert Horse' at Fort Irwin in California. The exercise lasted some six weeks and was the first time that the Multi Integrated Laser Engagement System or MILES was used on a major scale. In September 1980, the 2nd Battalion, 5th Cavalry Regiment was selected to field test the new XM-1 main battle tank that was named Abrams after General Creighton Abrams who succeeded General Westmoreland as the overall army commander in Vietnam.

Reforger exercises continued throughout the 1980s but on a reducing scale as the threat from the Warsaw Pact diminished. New equipment was absorbed such as the M-1 Abrams, the M-2 Bradley Infantry and M-3 Cavalry Fighting Vehicles as well as the MLRS (Multiple Launched Rocket System) and the AH-64 Apache attack helicopter. In addition, the HEMETT (Heavy Expanded Multi-purpose Tactical Truck) and the HMMWV (High Mobility Multi-purpose Wheeled Vehicle), better known as the Hummer, were

Left: An early production M-577 command vehicle is unloaded from a C-130 Hercules transport plane during a Reforger (Return of Forces to Germany) exercise in West Germany. During Exercise 'Reforger '83', 9,000 soldiers of the 1st Cavalry Division deployed to Holland, drew pre-positioned equipment and then moved to Germany where they conducted Exercise 'Certain Strike' on the North German Plains.

Below Left: The M-1 Abrams main battle tank entered service with the 1st Cavalry Division in 1980 and it remains the principal weapon system of the division to this day, albeit a much-enhanced uparmoured and upgunned model with the latest digital battle management equipment. The M-1 was named after General Creighton Abrams, the US Army commander in Vietnam, who was a great admirer of the First Air Cav and he once said, 'The big yellow patch does something to an individual that makes him a better soldier, a better team member, a better American than he otherwise would have been.'

introduced as was the equally important improvements in communications with the fielding of MSE (Mobile Subscriber Equipment) for secure voice and data transmission. This was augmented by SINGARS (Single Channel Ground to Air Communication System) which provides much enhanced security using frequency hopping technology. All this new equipment was assimilated by the division in large scale exercises at Fort Hood and at the National Training Center at Fort Irwin in the Mojave Desert. It was most opportune as the division received an order on 7 August 1990 for overseas deployment. The destination was Saudi Arabia following the Iraqi invasion of Kuwait five days before.

OPERATION 'DESERT SHIELD'/'DESERT SABER'

The personnel of 1st Cavalry Division flew to Dhahran on the shores of the Persian Gulf to await their equipment. Once it had arrived by sea, the division deployed to Assembly Area Horse some 160 miles westward where they acted as the principal counterattack force in the face of an Iraqi invasion of Saudi Arabia. After four months of intensive training in the desert, the 1st Cavalry Division was attached to VII US Corps for the coming offensive astride the Wadi al Batin. On 15 January 1991, a ferocious air assault was mounted against Iraq and its occupation forces in Kuwait. After a 38-day onslaught, the ground war was launched on 24 February. The mission of the 1st Cavalry Division was to conduct a feint attack up the Wadi al Batin as a diversion for the main attack by VII and XVIII Airborne Corps further westwards. Under a firestorm created by the MLRS of Battery A, 21st Field Artillery and the guns of the 3rd Battalion, 82nd Field Artillery, the 2nd 'Blackjack' Brigade advanced along the wadi ensnaring four Iraqi divisions as the main assault by VII Corps plunged into Iraq.

As the offensive developed, the 1st Cavalry Division struck the Iraqi 27th Infantry Division as well as elements of five other Iraqi divisions in an area that became known as the 'Ruqi Pocket'. By the afternoon of 27 February, the 1st Cavalry Division had advanced some 190 miles northeastwards slicing into the enemy's rear echelons. After 100 hours of combat, President George Bush ordered a ceasefire. The Iraqis had lost some 3,847 of their 4,280 tanks, over half of their 2,880 APCs and almost all of their 3,100 artillery pieces. It was a consummate victory but political considerations did not allow a hot pursuit to the capital Baghdad and the overthrow of Saddam Hussein. Over the coming years, elements of the 1st Cavalry Division were to return to Kuwait several times to conduct major desert exercises as a deterrent to further Iraqi aggression. Operation 'Vigilant Warrior' in 1994 was followed by Operation 'Vigilant Sentinel' in 1995 and Operation 'Intrinsic Action' in 1996 and 1997.

BOSNIAN PEACEKEEPERS

On its return from Kuwait to Fort Hood after the Gulf War, the 1st Cavalry Division was enlarged with the addition of the 3rd 'Greywolf' Battle Team and the Engineer Brigade to become the largest formation in the US Army. In November and December 1992, several of these new units were redesignated with famous historical titles of the 8th, 9th and 12th Cavalry Regiments. In its new configuration, the 1st Cavalry Division became the US Army's largest division and acted as a heavy armoured contingency force ready to deploy worldwide at short notice. It now comprised some 17,000 men and women with three manoeuvre brigades (Ironhorse, Blackjack, Greywolf), an aviation brigade (Warriors), an engineer brigade (Sappers), division artillery (Red Team) and division support command (Wagonmasters) plus an air defence battalion, a signal battalion, a military intelligence battalion and a military police company (Maverick).

Below: Among its many 'firsts', the First Team was the first division to field the M-2 Bradley Fighting Vehicle, the AH-64 Apache attack helicopter, the MLRS Multiple Launch Rocket System and the HMMWV Hummer. This model of the Bradley is the uparmoured M-2A2 that equipped the division just prior to the Gulf War of 1990/91.

On 16 April 1998, the 1st Cavalry Division was selected for peace support operations in Bosnia-Herzegovina to undertake the mission of 'Task Force Eagle'. After several months of intensive training, the 1st Cavalry Division under the command of Maj Gen Kevin P. Byrnes assumed authority of the Multi-National Division North from the 1st Armored Division – 'Old Ironsides'. The 1st Cavalry Division was the first to be deployed from the continental United States in a massive logistical operation as all previous units had come from Germany. The mission was to enforce the military provisions put forward by the Dayton Accords as part of Stabilization Force or SFOR 4 and 5. These were conducted by extensive patrolling in HUMVEEs and, occasionally, Bradley IFVs. At the same time, the Division Engineers cleared 80,000sq m of explosive ordnance and supervised the construction of $41m worth of base camp improvements. On 4 August 1999, the mission of Task Force Eagle was passed to the 10th Mountain Division with the last units of the 1st Cavalry Division returning to Fort Hood by 18 October.

Above: The UH-60 Black Hawk is the successor to the famous UH-1 Huey. In Bosnia, the Black Hawk was flown in support of the 1st Cavalry Division by the 3rd Battalion of the 229th Aviation Regiment, continuing a tradition that was forged over the jungles of South Vietnam, where the helicopter formation had its origins as Co C, the 'Widow Makers', of the 229th Assault Helicopter Bn. In Bosnia, the air assets of Task Force Eagle flew over 17,000 flying hours without mishap which represents one flying hour for every member of the 1st Cavalry Division.

OPERATION 'IRAQI FREEDOM'

The unfinished business of the First Gulf War was comprehensively rectified in March and April 2003 with the destruction of Saddam Hussein's odious regime. Between January and May 2004, the 1st Cavalry Division deployed to Iraq by air and sea to assume control of the Baghdad area with bases at Camp Victory North near the international airport as well as Camp Cooke, Camp Dragoon, Camp War Eagle, Camp Muleskinner and inside the 'Green Zone' headquarters enclave of the Coalition Forces. After leaving its Abrams MBTs at Fort Hood, it was now classified as a Light Motorized, Task Oriented, Cavalry Division and equipped with M-2 Bradley Fighting Vehicles, M-1114 armoured HUMVEEs and the M-1117 Guardian Armored Security Vehicle (ASV-150) to undertake its security mission in the capital and its environs.

With attached units from the Army National Guard, the 1st Cavalry Division assumed responsibility for the Baghdad area from the 1st Armored Division on 15 April 2004. From the outset, operations have been conducted against the al-Mahdi army militia based in the Shiite slums of Sadr City, formerly Saddam City. Repeated and relentless attacks against the 1st Cavalry Division have continued since its arrival in theatre resulting in a steady stream of casualties. Up to the time of the transfer of sovereignty to the interim Iraqi government on 28 June 2004, 49 members of the 1st Cavalry Division had been killed in action undertaking Operation 'Iraqi Freedom'. The price of freedom remains high.

REFERENCE

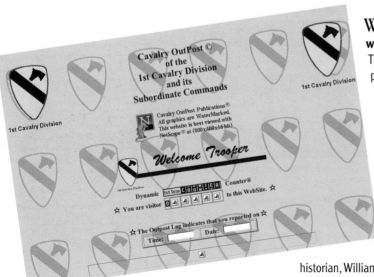

WEBSITES

www.rolling-thunder.org.uk

The premier UK reenactment group for the era (see above photograph).

www.first-team.us

This official website of the 1st Cavalry Division (Airmobile) is an outstanding source of information on the division from its earliest lineage to current operations in Iraq. It has extensive coverage of all aspects of the division's history from the order of battle to the words of the traditional marching song of the 7th Cavalry – the Garry Owen. This 'Spearhead' volume has drawn extensively from this website with the kind permission of the divisional historian, William Harry Boudreau, and Cavalry Outpost Publications.

Wm. Harry Boudreau is also the author of the current divisional history:

1st Cavalry Division – A Spur Ride Through The 20th Century, From Horses To The Digital Battlefield; Turner Publishing Company, Paducah K, 2002.

BIBLIOGRAPHY

The 1st Air Cavalry Division Vietnam Volume 1
August 1965 to December 1969
This highly illustrated 296-page volume was published by the division in 1970. It provides a general history of the division's activities during the time period stated but its real worth is in the accounts of the various units and sub-units within the division interspersed with some excellent photographs and illustrations.

The Vietnam Experience
Multi-part series by Boston Publishing Company.
This series of almost 40 volumes published during the 1980s is a comprehensive and authoritative history of the conflict covering virtually every aspect of the war. It is an outstanding source of reference.

Brennan, Matthew: *Brennan's War – Vietnam 1965-1969*; Presidio, 1985.
Matthew Brennan was one of those elite helicopter pilots that enlisted at an early age and had an extraordinary flying career in Vietnam where he made over 400 combat air assaults with the 'Headhunters' of the 9th Cavalry. This searing first-hand account gives a vivid impression of the war from the helicopter pilot's seat. So does Matthew Brennan's subsequent volume *Hunter Killer Squadron – Vietnam 1965-1972* that is a collection of personal stories of the men that made up the elite formation – the 1st Squadron, 9th Cavalry.

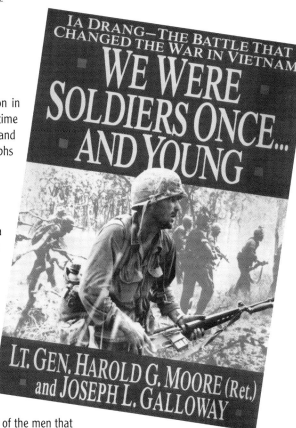

Johnson, Lawrence H., III: *Winged Sabers – The Air Cavalry in Vietnam*; Stackpole Books, 1990.
This excellent book gives a comprehensive overview of the development and operations of the Air Cavalry in Vietnam, together with the aircraft, equipment, unit histories and uniforms as well as their distinctive insignia. It is profusely illustrated throughout with remarkable photographs drawn from many sources, particularly those of veterans.

Mertel, Col Kenneth D., US Army (Ret): *Year of the Horse: Vietnam – 1st Air Cavalry in the Highlands 1965-1967*; Schiffer Military History, 1997. Colonel Kenneth Mertel was the commander of the 1st Battalion, 8th Cavalry and the *Year of the Horse: Vietnam* is a day-by-day account of the exploits of the 'Jumping Mustangs' during the initial years of the Vietnam War. The book has some especially useful appendices on the airmobility in Vietnam and on the air assault into Cambodia in 1970.

Moore, Lt Gen (Ret.) Harold G. and Galloway, Joseph L.: *We Were Soldiers Once…And Young Ia Drang: The Battle That Changed The War In Vietnam*; Random House, 1992.
This book is the definitive account of the battle of the Ia Drang Valley written by the commander of the 1st Battalion, 7th Cavalry, Hal Moore, and by the UPI journalist Joseph Galloway who accompanied the Sky Soldiers into the battle zone as a first-hand witness. The book includes interesting coverage from the North Vietnamese point of view as well and it formed the basis of the film

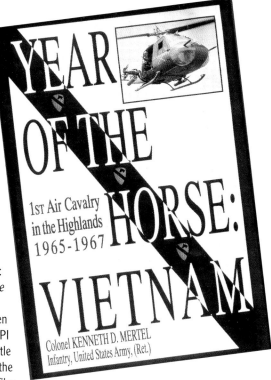

We Were Soldiers Once with Mel Gibson portraying Lt Col Hal Moore at the battle of the Ia Drang Valley.

Shelby L. Stanton: *Anatomy of a Division – 1st Cav in Vietnam*; Presidio, 1987.
Shelby L. Stanton is one of the foremost military historians of the Vietnam War with numerous works on the conflict to his credit. His *Anatomy of a Division* remains an exemplary concise history of the 1st Cavalry Division (Airmobile) from its inception to its return from South East Asia and its reconfiguration as an armoured division.

Shelby L. Stanton: *The Rise and Fall of an American Army – US Ground Forces in Vietnam, 1965-1973*; Presidio, 1985.
As a combat veteran of the Vietnam War, Shelby Stanton is highly qualified to recount the achievements of the US Army on the battlefields of South Vietnam from the initial optimism of the early years to the times of disillusion as the process of withdrawal took place. This important book sets the essential background to the overall conduct of the ground war with numerous references to the 1st Cavalry Division (Airmobile).

Shelby L. Stanton: *Vietnam Order of Battle*; US News Books, 1981.
Any serious student of the Vietnam War must have Shelby Stanton's magisterial and encyclopedic reference work *Vietnam Order of Battle* on his bookshelves. Recently republished, this 416-page compendium covers the entire organisation, structure and operations of US and Allied ground units in Vietnam from 1961 to 1973.

DVD

We Were Heroes – 1st Cavalry Division (Airmobile) Vietnam
DVD 9313 Madacy Entertainment Group Inc 2002
This three-DVD boxed set features archival footage of the arrival of the 1st Cavalry Division (Airmobile) in South Vietnam and the early battles including the Ia Drang and the A Shau Valley. Other features include helicopter operations in Vietnam, air mobility as well as a piece on Know Your Enemy about the Viet Cong.

1st CAVALRY DIVISION (AIRMOBILE) IN VIETNAM TIMELINE

1965

14 August: First 1st Cavalry Division combat troops sent to Vietnam.

27 August: 1st Cavalry Division advance party landed at An Khe, Vietnam.

18 September: First combat of Vietnam War for 1st Cavalry Troopers in Op 'Shiny Bayonet'.

19 October: Op 'Pleiku' begins.

1 November: 1-9 Cavalry fights hospital battle.

3 November: 1-9 Cavalry ambushes 66th NVA Regiment at LZ Betty.

14 November: 7th Cavalry air assaults into LZ X-Ray; 2nd Lt Walter J. Marm, A-1/7 Cavalry earns the Medal of Honor; Capt Edward W. Freeman, A-229th AHB, earns the Medal of Honor.

17 November: 2-7 Cavalry, Company A, 1-5 Cavalry battle at LZ Albany.

19 November: Op 'Silver Bayonet' begins.

26 November: Op 'Pleiku' ends.

17 December: Op 'Clean House' begins.

31 December: Op 'Clean House' ends.

1966

25 January: Op 'Masher/White Wing' begins.

6 March: Op 'Masher/White Wing' ends.

25 March: Op 'Lincoln House' begins.

8 April: Op 'Lincoln House' ends.

4 May: Op 'Davy Crockett' begins.

10 May: Op 'Davy Crockett' ends.

16 May: Op 'Crazy Horse' begins.

18 May: SSgt Jimmy G. Stewart, B-2/12 Cavalry earns the Medal of Honor.

21 May: Sgt David C. Dolby, B-1/8 Cavalry earns the Medal of Honor.

5 June: Op 'Crazy Horse' ends.

19 June: Op 'Nathan Hale' begins.

1 July: Op 'Nathan Hale' ends.

2 August: Op 'Paul Revere II' begins.

15 August: Op 'Paul Revere II' ends at the battle of Hill 534.

25 July: Op 'Byrd' begins.

13 September: Op 'Thayer I' begins.

21 September: PFC Billy L. Lauffer, C-2/5 Cavalry earns the Medal of Honor.

1 October: Op 'Thayer I' ends.

2 October: Op 'Irving' begins, over 2,000 enemy prisoners of war captured.

24 October: Op 'Irving' ends.

26 October: Op 'Thayer II' begins. 31 October: Op 'Paul Revere IV' begins.

1 December: PFC Lewis Albanese, B-5/7 Cavalry earns the Medal of Honor.

27 December: Op 'Paul Revere IV' ends; SSG Delbert O. Jennings, C-1/12 Cavalry earns The Medal of Honor.

1967

30 January: Op 'Byrd' ends.

12 February: Op 'Thayer II' ends; Op 'Pershing' begins.

16 February: PFC James H. Monroe, C-1/8 Cavalry earns the Medal of Honor.

20 March: Sp5 Charles C. Hagemeister, A-1/5 earns the Medal of Honor.

7 April: Op 'LeJeune' begins.

16 April: Sp4 George A. Ingalls, A-2/5 Cavalry earns the Medal of Honor.

22 April: Op 'LeJeune' ends.

21 June: Sp5 Edgal L. McWethy Jr., B-1/5 Cavalry earns the Medal of Honor; Sp4 Carmel B. Harvey Jr., B-1/5 Cavalry earns the Medal of Honor.

1 August: Op 'Song Re' begins.

20 August: Op 'Song Re' ends.

2 October: Op 'Wheller/Wallowa' begins.

15 December: Sgt Allen James Lynch, D-1/12 Cavalry earns the Medal of Honor.

1968

12 January: Sgt William D. Port, C-5/7 earns the Medal of Honor.

21 January: Op 'Pershing' ends.

22 January: Op 'Pershing II' begins; Op 'Jeb Stuart' begins.

25 January: Op 'Wheller/Wallowa' ends.

31 January: CW2 Fredrick Ferguson, C-227 Aviation Battalion earns the Medal of Honor; North Vietnamese and Viet Cong launch 'Tet Offensive' at Hue.

18 February: Op 'Pershing II' ends.

22 February: North Vietnamese and Viet Cong driven from the city of Hue.

31 March: Op 'Jeb Stuart' ends.

1 April: Op 'Pegasus/Lamson 207' begins.

15 April: Op 'Pegasus/Lamson 207' ends.

19 April: Op 'Delaware/Lamson 216' begins.

25 April: Capt James M. Sprayberry, D-5/7 Cavalry earns the Medal of Honor.

4 May: 1st Lt Douglas B. Fournet, B-1/7 Cavalry earns the Medal of Honor.

8 May; Op 'Concordia Square' begins.

17 May: Op 'Delaware/Lamson 217' ends; Op 'Jeb Stuart III' begins; Op 'Concordia Square' ends.

28 June: Sp4 Hector Santiago Colon, B-5/7 Cavalry earns Medal of Honor.

11 September: Op 'Comanche Falls' begins.

3 November: Op 'Jeb Stuart III' ends.

7 November: Op 'Comanche Falls' ends.

12 November: Op 'Toan Thang' begins.

15 November: Op 'Liberty Canyon' ends.

3 December: Sgt John N. Holcomb, D-2/7 Cavalry earns the Medal of Honor.

1969

23 January: Op 'Montana Scout/Raider' begins.

16 February: Op 'Toan Thang' ends.

21 March: Sp4 Donald R. Johnston, D-1/8 Cavalry earns the Medal of Honor.

2 June: 1st Lt Robert L. Poxon, B-1/9 Cavalry earns the Medal of Honor.

18 July: Sgt Rodney J. Evans, D-1/12 earns the Medal of Honor.

14 September: Sgt Donald S. Skidgel, D-1/9 Cavalry earns the Medal of Honor.

2 December: 2nd Lt Robert R. Leisy, B-1/8 Cavalry earns the Medal of Honor.

1970

10 February: Sp4 John P. Baca, D-1/12 Cavalry earns the Medal of Honor.

1 April: Sgt Peter C. Lemon, E-2/8 Cavalry earns the Medal of Honor.

1 May: Op 'Thon Thang Fish Hook' begins; First Team enters Cambodia.

29 June: Op 'Thon Thang Fish Hook' ends.

1971

26 February: Cpt Jon Edward Swanson, B-1/9 Cavalry earns the Medal of Honor.

26 March: 1st Team stands down in Vietnam.

5 May: 1st Cavalry Division assigned to Fort Hood, Texas.

1972

26 June: Op 'Keystone Pheasant' begins.

29 June: 3rd Brigade departs Vietnam.

1973

28 January: Cease-fire in Vietnam begins.

28 March: US ground troops leave Vietnam.

INDEX